By: Richard Monroe Bennett

The Life of A Player... ®

(Including my years with PLAYBOY!)

The Library of Congress has catalogued this book as follows:

Publication Data

Richard Monroe Bennett

The Life of a Player

TXu 1-863-658

Acknowledgment

In great appreciation to Manetta Niessen, without her help this book could not have happened.

Thanks,

Rich

D0724561

The Life of A Player...

By: RICHARD MONROE BENNETT

CONTENTS

The Life of A Player... ®

By: RICHARD MONROE BENNETT *(Including my years with PLAYBOY!)*

This Is My Story

Chapter 1: Early History

A little early history: Three brothers arrived in James Town, Virginia, from England in 1622, changing their name from Bennet with one "T" to Bennett with two "T's".

Starting cotton farms and different kinds of businesses all over the South, my father's family settled in Greensboro, North Carolina, where he was born. His father and mother owned a local general store and lived comfortably with two sisters and three brothers. My father's parents loved music and had all their children take up an instrument. My father selected the trumpet. He would drive the others crazy with his practicing, compared to the strings and piano his brothers and sisters studied. After high school, he became a professional musician and was quickly given the nickname of Easy Ed because of his easygoing personality. He played with some of the biggest names in the business at that time, including Slats Randall and Don Bigelow. One of the singers who was with the band was Helen

Babe Kane. She inspired the character of Betty Boop in 1930 with her dancing, singing style, and a catchphrase of "Boop-oop-a-doop"! My father fell in love with another beauty at a gig

in Brooklyn, New York (my mother). That's when Babe Kane gave my father a picture of herself with a personalized message to my dad. *"To Eddie: With my very best wishes. Remember me, please - Babe."* With a *"PS (No more **Pink**)"* *The meaning – after gigs they would go to the beach and watch the sun come up, which they wouldn't be enjoying together anymore....*

Ginger Rogers was another vocalist he dated, until she left for Hollywood. After all of his trumpet playing days, he blew a lung. He then had a hard time finding a job. Doctor Krenz, our family doctor, would come to our home when needed and became a part of the family. He gave my father a job at his farm on Long Island, until my father found an opening with a company called ADT, located in the Village of New York City. This relieved a lot of pressure on the family. The job led to a long relationship with a growing company. At this same time I was born in Brooklyn, New York, on December 29, 1933, and lived there for one year. We then moved to Queens, New York, to an apartment with one bath, two bedrooms, dining room, living room and kitchen. I have an older brother, Edwin Jr., and two younger sisters, Barbara and Pat. I didn't spend too much time with my brother. He did brainy things and didn't fit into my world of trouble making.

The infamous Genovese family owned the apartment buildings. I can remember the one time I went with my mother to pay our rent, which we only had part of. We arrived at the empty apartment, which was set up to collect rent with one desk and a big burly man behind it. My mother was nervous and didn't know what to expect. She presented the problem to the man. I think she brought me along as a sympathetic gesture, but to her surprise the man couldn't have been nicer. He understood and said she could make it up the next month. It seemed the family didn't want any problems and were willing to help all their 200 apartment renters, so the Genovese family wasn't so bad after all.

I still wonder how the six of us fit in a two-bedroom, one bath apartment. Those were the good old days. I would love to see how the kids of today would handle that with no air conditioning, television, phones, mobile phones, or iPads!

One of our neighbors worked for Coca-Cola and would give us jackets that said Coca-Cola on them. (Green jackets with red letters.) They were really neat. So in return, we made up a song that went like this, "Pepsi-Cola, stinky drink, pour it down the kitchen sink, tastes like vinegar, looks like ink, Pepsi-Cola is a stinky drink." Our neighbor loved it!

The War

When I was about 8 years old, shopping in the city with my mother, it was just a day like any other day except for one thing. It happened on our return. I was holding my mother's hand, going down the stairs at Queens Plaza subway station. All of a sudden, a man came running by repeatedly hollering, "They bombed Pearl Harbor, they bombed Pearl Harbor." I didn't know what the heck he was saying until I looked at my mother's face. She was very frightened, which made me feel the same way. That's when I started finding out about other parts of the world. It was a heck of a way to start finding out, on December 7th, 1941! After that we had stamps for gas and food that were allotted by the size of your family. They were

3

like gold and we were careful with their use. To help in the war effort, all of us kids would collect metal and throw it over the fence at the local church knowing that we were helping to fight those bad Japs and Germans.

My father had a storage bin in the cellar of the apartment complex that he had made into a ham radio station. His call letters were W-2MZU. He would talk to ships at sea and other radio hams. He spent a lot of time there. He set up a speaker system so that he could hear everything that was going on in the apartment just overhead. When it was time for dinner, my mother would call into the speakers, "Ed, it's time for dinner." He had all kinds of little gimmicks. One I remember was he would have us hold a fluorescent bulb in our hand and walk slowly toward the 6-foot stack of radios and receivers. The bulb would start lighting up as we got closer. That was scary. I also remember using a needle and a piece of crystal and picking up a radio station. How cool is that? One day the FBI came in and closed down the storage bin by putting a lock and tape across the door. That was so exciting for us kids. We would bring our friends to see how the FBI closed up the bin. That gave us some feeling of importance. After that, my father became a civil defense man. I had some special times with him, going on his practice air raids. His area was at LaGuardia Airport, where he would call in on his mobile unit, clearing the area. He also had gas masks, which I used when I had to babysit for my younger sister, Barbara. I always wondered what they were used for?

My mother taught dancing part-time. She also taught us kids so that we wouldn't be wallflowers. This would come in handy later on in life. She raised us as Catholics and decided to send me to Sunday school. At school I was talking to one of the other kids, when out of nowhere a nun hit me on the hands with a ruler. That was the last time I went to that school! I guess that's one of the reasons why I'm an ex-communicated Catholic.

A Few Strong Memories

Movies were important in those days because you would try to mimic the good guys. The right way is the best way sometimes, unlike today's pictures where the bad guy often gets away with murder. Tyrone Power was my favorite actor hero, especially in the original Zorro. I would dream about it. Another hero of mine was Jackie Robinson. I even tried to run like him, pigeon-toed. Talking about pigeons, we used to climb up under the train bridges at night with a flashlight shining it into the eyes of a pigeon, paralyzing it so all you had to do was grab it. Then my buddy, Blimpy, would build a fire and quickly pull the pigeon's head off, clean and de-feather it, preparing to put it on a stick for cooking over the fire. The juice would run off, making our taste buds burst with hunger. It tasted great!

Another time, I had a toothache. My mother, being resourceful, heard that there was a one-dollar dental clinic, at St. John's Hospital, so she gave me a dollar. I flattened out a penny (for the subway which cost a nickel); and went on my way. I waited in a long line in the basement of the hospital, scared stiff! When the moment arrived, the irritated dentist said, "Well, do you want it pulled or filled?" I gave him my dollar bill and said, "Pull it!" Little did I know that it was my permanent tooth that he pulled? (Live and learn!) There certainly is a BIG difference in prices back then and now.

My First Hospital Stay

While playing touch tackle in the schoolyard, which was concrete, I somehow broke the little toe on my left foot, although I didn't realize it at the time. Finally, with athlete's foot, and my toe-swollen blue, I developed osteomyelitis (bone infection). I had to be hospitalized. I was put into a room with four beds. While preparing me for my operation, I had to have shots to keep the infection from spreading. While my mother and father were at my bedside, the nurse came in to give me a shot in my rear end. She told me to turn over. I prepared my body for the penetration of the needle by tightening up my rear end. The nurse thrust the needle, and it bent at impact. My mother couldn't stop laughing. The nurse asked, "is he superman?" She made up for it with a sharper needle. Then it came time for the operation. They gave me a local so I could watch the whole thing, as they picked out black infected bone and sewed it up. It's funny how the human brain can't accept watching your body being cut, and feeling no pain. Welcome to the world of surgery. While recuperating that day in my hospital bed, I noticed the man across from me, who was in serious condition, having trouble swallowing his soup that the nurse was giving him by spoon. She came up with an idea to use a glass straw, dipping it into the soup, putting her thumb on the top to hold the soup in the straw, then releasing it deeper into the patient's mouth. She asked him, "is that okay?" He nodded. I was watching the whole thing. That night I was awakened by lots of commotion. The gentleman across from me was in trouble. The doctor ordered a pump. They started pumping the fluid that was in his lungs. The doctor asked, "where did all this liquid come from?" In spite of all the doctor's efforts, the gentleman died. And I knew why. (That was my first stay at a hospital.)

A Day In Central Park

Blimpie and I would go to Central Park on rainy days to fish, because there would be less people and the police wouldn't bother us. We would flatten out our penny and off we would go. We found a nice place, under the trees on the water's edge that kept the rain to a minimum. While fishing with bobbers and worms, a rowboat appeared with a man and woman in it. They pulled up to us and the gentleman asked what we were fishing for? The woman looked bored and uncomfortable under her umbrella, but she was beautiful. Blimpie said to the gentleman: "Don't I know you from the movies?" He replied" "yes, I'm shooting a picture now with Danny Kaye. It's called "Wonderman".   We asked: "What's your name?" He replied: "Steve Cochran."   (He was one of the top actors at that time.) He continued: "I play the heavyweight boxing champ who has to beat up Danny Kaye." "The kids won't like me for that", he said sadly. It was fun meeting and talking with him, but as Hollywood goes... he ended up, in later years, dying on a boat lost at sea for ten days off the coast of Guatemala with three young women on board with his dead body. He was only 48. Tough way to go!

Trouble

Blimpy and I were always getting into trouble. One-time, two plain-clothes policemen in an unmarked car stopped us. We had slingshots and we were shooting at birds in a private housing area. Someone must have called them, because they immediately grabbed us and started roughing us up, and asking us questions about where we lived and where our parents worked. I told them that I didn't know exactly where in the city he worked. (True.) They didn't like my answer. The cop who was holding Blimpy said to him, "if your friend runs away I won't hesitate shooting him." The other cop who was holding me thought I was a wise guy and slapped me around and said, "get in the car," but I wouldn't go, no matter what they did. Finally they figured they had scared us enough. They let us go. We were next to a train trestle track, which we ran up looking down on the two cops standing next to their car. I grabbed a rock and threw it down at them. We ran before I could see if I made a hit or not.

Victory Day – May 9th, 1945

After World War II was over, the heavy influx of the military coming home was overwhelming, so the government had to build small housing for them called Quonset huts. One of the locations for them was near LaGuardia Airport, not far from my apartment. It was a maze of them cramped together. My favorite uncle, Phil, and family were part of it, and I visited them quite often. What stood out in my memory was the massive amount of white laundry, hanging on clotheslines between the huts. We gave it a nickname calling it "the white flag area."

The Army also had to unload all their equipment, so they set up warehouses in Queens; with sections for clothing, radio equipment and all motorized vehicles. My father had a ball in the radio section where you could buy things for practically nothing. My mother took my brother and me to the clothing section, where we picked up winter Army jackets that were real neat. There was also the section in the back, which was fenced in, that held all the jeeps and motorized vehicles. I noticed that there was a lack of security, so Blimpy and I took advantage of the situation, sneaking in at night, trying to find a vehicle that would start and going for a joyride around the lot. Those were the days!

Our playgrounds were the subway tunnels. For amusement, we would flatten out a penny with a rock to fit the turn slot of the subway. It would get us from Queens to Brooklyn's Coney Island, with a transfer. We also played tag in the subway tunnels that had little light; 60-watt bulbs, scattered around the area giving us more confidence in

8

entering. When a train came by at full throttle, we pressed against the wall in small cutouts. Sparks from the electrified third rail glittered in the dark along with a clicking noise that hurt your ears from the steel wheels. The flashing of the lights from the windows of the passing train made it look like a thunderstorm. It was like the train was trying to pull us out of the cutout in the wall; scary but exhilarating! Jumping over the third rail gave us an exciting feeling. The train engineers must have been shocked when they saw us running around in the darkness of the tunnels illuminated by the train's headlights as it sped by. Another exciting game was playing tag in the sewers. Talk about scary, but you never wanted your gang to know you were afraid! There is nothing like the underground world of New York City. Outside the tunnels: we also rode our bikes over the girders on the unfinished Brooklyn Queens Expressway, which was halted because of World War II. On a dare, we would hang by our fingers from the Triboro Bridge, while across the way, patients in the sanitarium were watching us through the bars as we hung precariously. They would wave and holler at us. I didn't know what they were saying, but they probably thought that we should be in with them! There were two gangs on our street; the older guys ranged in age from 16 to 18, ours was 12 to 15. We were known as the 49'ers, because of living on 49th street. The older boys would arrange fights between us by getting one younger kid to fight another. One time I got sucked into one, which was against the younger brother of one of the older gang. I knew I could beat him, but the older guys wouldn't let me. Every time I got the best of him, they would pull me away and we would start again - to their amusement. Finally it was over! If they didn't slap you around, you were lucky. Another time I learned a lesson from this redheaded kid who was being bullied around by one of the older guys he was being forced to fight. The redhead said, "you may beat me, but I will get one shot in that will hurt you." The big kid thought about it and backed off. It worked! Another trouble making thing was to stand at the end of 48th street, our rivals. We would start throwing rocks down the street and run, but this one night, during one of those rock-throwing incidents, some guy came running out of his apartment and fired a shot. It hit the cement sidewalk and ricocheted, hitting me just above my right ankle. I panicked; not knowing how bad the wound was I ran back home. Luckily there was no one there. I went into the bathroom. My sneaker was filled with blood. I started to clean it up. It was only a flesh wound. I wrapped it with toilet paper, dunking my sneaker into the toilet bowl, flushing the blood away. I never had the bullet hole stitched, so it left a lasting scar. I walked with a limp and told everyone that I sprained my ankle. My family never found out about it. Our gang had nothing much to do, so we would think of things. One night we decided to break into a school, taking some paintings from the auditorium, and bust them up. I guess it was our way of rebelling against authority. We eventually got caught and had to go to the 114th precinct with my father. We ended up paying a fine. Gang peer pressure, if you didn't go with them you were looked down upon and even kicked out of their protection.

Against The Wall

Belonging to a city gang can be dangerous, if you wander too far from their protection. That's a mistake I made when I left myself alone in an open lot at the end of my street. All of a sudden six or seven cronies approached me from 48th street, our rivals. They were looking for one of our gang who was always getting into trouble away from our group. They asked me if I knew him and where he was? I said I didn't know. That's when the leader of the group pointed to one of his boys playing with his knife, and said he would cut you with no problem if you lie to us. I started backing up against the concrete wall that was behind me. Everyone would throw bottles at the wall, getting rid of their frustration, thus leaving a floor of glass. I could feel and hear the glass crunching under my feet letting the gang know that I was retreating. That's not good, so I picked up a broken bottle and held it out in front of me. I felt like a trapped rat and had nothing to lose. To my surprise, that stopped them from moving forward. It was like no one wanted to make the first move. Finally, the gang leader said, I like this guy, and they all retreated from the lot. I stood there, almost pissing in my pants. It's just another lesson I learned growing up on the streets.

After that, my parents decided to send me to work on my Uncle Doc's tobacco farm in Greensboro, N.C., for two months when school was out. This decision was made to get me out of the city.

Chapter 2: Disciplinary Move - 1946

I was put on a train with a sleeper. I was 13 years old. It was my first trip out of the city. My mother dressed me in a light blue suit that wrinkled at a glance. Of course I slept in it because I was afraid I would miss my stop. You can imagine what I looked like when I met my uncle Doc and Aunt Cleo at the train station in Greensboro! They didn't even notice. After all, they were tobacco farmers! I thought that this farm life was going to be boring, but I was in for a surprise.

One of the first things my uncle wanted to know was what I liked for breakfast. I told him "Wheaties, Breakfast of Champions." He didn't know what that was, so we went to the local store. No one there had ever heard of it, but the owner said he would look it up in his book. At last he found it! The only thing was, we had to order a case. My uncle said, "Okay, I'll order a case a week for two months." At the end of most weeks, the whole family would be eating Wheaties, just to get ready for the next case. That's how I came to be called Richard Wheaties Bennett. Sleeping quarters were different also. The mattresses and pillows were made up of burlap, hay with a pan at bedside so we didn't have to make that trip to the outhouse in the dark.

Farm life taught me a lot, including how to spay a dog. Which means removing the ovaries from an animal. My 80 year old Uncle King, a burly, bearded man, who could do just about anything, would only operate on a dog when the moon was full; and never lost one! How he started this process was to get a board on which to tie the dog down, including the mouth. With a penknife, cut a two-inch slit in the dog's side, with no anesthetic, pulling out the stomach. My uncle said to me, "you couldn't do this to a human", while putting the stomach on the dog's side, cutting off something and shoving it back into the open slit and sewing it up. My cousin got sick during this procedure. I was just mesmerized by the whole thing. The dog was then put into a doghouse for a couple of days. When they let her out, she started to ride all the other dogs. (Maybe it's something I can use in later life? (Ha!)

My uncle used blacks to help him during harvest time. He would pay them one dollar a day. That was the going rate, plus lunch, which most of the other farmers didn't do. He also had help from the local authorities. When he had heavy work to be done, they would bring a chain gang with striped pants and shirts, chained together with a guard standing by with a double-barreled shotgun. Curiously, I would ask them what they were in for? I think they tried to scare me by telling me murderous stories. From that I learned quickly that jails weren't for me.

While I was on the farm, my father came down to put electricity into a house his mother had bought after my grandfather's death. He asked me to help him. My father was a " jack-of-all-trades and a master of none." That's where I learned a lot about wiring homes. It would come in handy later on in life. My uncle's farm had no electricity, running water, or bathrooms, and just a well for water. I learned to milk cows and store the milk in the creek to keep it cold. I was also given a job driving the 10-foot sled filled with tobacco that the pickers in the field would fill and I would return the full load back to the cooking barn. (Sounds easy.) I didn't know if the guys gave me this horse on purpose or not, but when I came to a puddle in the furrow, the horse stopped. You could see that something was wrong, he couldn't figure out how to get around the puddle, because of the tobacco stalks on each side of him. All of a sudden, his hindquarters went down. That's when I knew I was in trouble. He was getting ready to jump over this 5-foot puddle. Sure as hell, he jumped and dragged me 30 feet, tearing down dozens of stalks and turning over the sled and emptying it. That was embarrassing! Now that I had experience and skill in driving the sled back to the barn where the women were tying the tobacco leaves on sticks to get them ready for hanging in the cooking barn, I was supposed to drive the sled close to their bench to make it easier for them to have access to the tobacco leaves. This time I got too close and took the 8-foot long bench out from under them, putting them all on the ground. How bad can it be?

The next step was to hang the tied tobacco up in the barn five tiers high, separated just right to make them cook to an even golden brown. This was critical when it came time to price at auction. It took three days and nights of the constant fires to achieve the finished product. One night it was my turn to stay with my uncle Doc. We slept on cots under the open skies with the sounds of crickets and June bugs singing in the trees like an orchestra trying to blend together. During the night, I could see my uncle getting up to put more logs into the furnace, keeping the temperature just right. Morning finally came with the sun burning my eyes. Rubbing the sleep from them, I could see my uncle strangely looking over at me. He said, in a firm voice. "Stay still." I froze at his command. He got up, picked up a stick and walked slowly towards me. With a wave of his stick, he knocked away a copperhead snake that was under my cot. I never had that problem back in New York!

There were lots of things to do preparing for the tobacco season. Many trees had to be cut into logs and stacked, like teepees to dry out, until it was time to retrieve them for burning in the tobacco barn furnace. We found it was a perfect place for bees, wasps and snakes to hide, so we did a lot of running. At that time, I remember my uncle telling me to run for the nearest bush and get into it when the bees attacked. It worked! Another thing, before the season, they would plant watermelons in different areas around the tobacco fields. When we would take a break on those hot days, we would venture into the woods, and retrieve one, burying our faces into it. What a natural refreshing feeling. Things were well thought out. After the tobacco was cooked, they would store it in the attic of an old barn, before taking it to market.

Rat Hunt

The barn was half sunk in the ground from rats making paths underground. The rats would also make nests in the tobacco leaves, ruining them. So we had to have a Rat Hunt.

My uncle Doc told me to stand near this hole in the floor and when a rat came to it, hit him with this bat. He also told me a rat always slows up just before entering a hole. That was my time to strike! The five dogs were getting excited. It seems they knew what was about to happen. One of my cousins went up into the attic and started hitting the metal roofing that was put there for just this purpose. The noise scared the rats and they started coming out of the walls. Most of them ran to my hole. I started swinging! The dogs would pick them up and run out the door. One of the rat's bit one of the dog's tongue while he had it in his mouth, ripping it. The dog yipped and the rat fell to the floor. The dog grabbed him up again and ran off with it. It was fun and I felt rewarded with five notches on my bat.

The dogs were also used for hunting in winter. We had to exercise them by taking them possum hunting in the summer. Once they had a possum treed, someone had to go up the tree and shake it loose, so the dogs could make their kill. I was elected. I didn't want anyone to think I was scared, so I went up, crawling out onto the limb while the possum was hissing and showing it's teeth. I felt like I had been shaking that limb forever! Thank God he finally fell! The dogs jumped on the possum and killed it, but didn't eat it. My uncle told me that they only had a spoonful of blood in them and that was why. (Boy am I learning a lot!)

I learned about mules, horses, and how mules are smarter. You say "Gee," they go right, you say "Haw," they go left. I also learned about slaughtering pigs, salting them and hanging them in the well house so the meat didn't spoil.

Crows were a problem. They were so bad that the town of Greensboro, N.C., was giving twenty-five cents for crow's feet. They were so much of a pest to farmers, especially in cornfields. They would gather in one particular tree and if the scout birds saw anyone, they would signal the others and they would fly off. My Uncle Doc wired the tree with dynamite and when they gathered, he blew the top of the tree off! We collected a lot of crow's feet!

Another time, late at night, there was a loud commotion out in the chicken barn. My cousin, Clyde, went out and found a black snake with a half swallowed chicken in its mouth. Poor snake, didn't have a chance. He shot him!

Church

My uncle and aunt sang in the choir at church. Sometimes they would get me up there with them, which I hated! Some of the songs I still remember. One in particular, it goes like this:

> *"Life's Evening Sun is sinking*
> *low, a few more days, and I*
> *must go, to meet the deeds that*
> *I have done. Life's evening sun*
> *is sinking low."*
>
> (I guess it means something.)

The church would have a picnic, once a month with fried chicken, ice cream, and chocolate cake; a young boy's dream. I loved that part of church, but there were things I didn't like. On Sunday I was put into a Bible study class. We all had to take our turn reading verses aloud. When it came to me, the fear was unbelievable and I couldn't even speak. The reason was because of an experience I had in third grade. We had to read in front of the class. It was my turn to read. I came to a word I didn't know, a small word. The teacher helped me out by telling me it was "elephant." I repeated it.

16

The whole class laughed to my total embarrassment. This would have a lasting effect on my life. I would hide in the back of the class and play hooky every chance I could to avoid this problem. After that Sunday school experience, I would go fishing on Sundays. My aunt would say, "The devil's going to get your hook!" (He never did!)

My Friend Pete

On the farm we were kept quite busy, but still, their were slow times also. I became attached to this little just-born baby chicken. I named him Pete. He thought I was his mother. He would follow me everywhere until I had to put him on my shoulder when I could see he couldn't keep up, which he loved. After he was about a month or so older, we would occasionally make a trip to the mailbox, which was about a quarter of a mile down a dirt road. He would follow me until he started wobbling. I knew he was tired, so I picked him up. I had this feeling of love, as I was mumbling baby-like words, putting him on my shoulder. When we returned to the house, Pete would stretch out on the sandy ground with one wing stretched out in a sunny spot that was coming through the tree leaves. I, being a 13-year-old kid, thought that this was so much fun. I adopted another baby chick but this one wasn't like Pete. He ran from me. While we were out under the tree, I was chasing the little one around the bench, which I jumped onto trying to retrieve it; but it ran back under the bench, so I jumped back off. It was one of the most shocking feelings that I would have in my short life. Pete was just sunbathing with his wing stretched out enjoying the warmth of the sun like he usually did, until my heel landed on him, crushing his head. He started jumping around, just like a chicken that had his head cut off. I couldn't believe my eyes, rushing to him and picking him up gently with my two hands, hoping that someone

17

could fix him. Finally he stopped moving. My uncle Doc did all he could, the whole family loved Pete also. I cried all night with Pete in my hands, and the next morning, I put Pete into a matchbox and buried him in a nice sunny spot, with a chain cross over it; but how do you accept killing something you love? (This was my introduction to real life.)

Lumber Camp

My Uncle Doc had a floating lumber camp also. This means they set up camp on leased acres and cut down certain trees, cutting them up into railroad ties on site with large bladed saws and generators that had to be started by a guy named Superman. Once he cranked that large thing and got it started, we knew it was time to start working. We had a Caterpillar to pull the cut trees to the cutting area. My Uncle gave me a chance to drive, steering with hand brakes. It was like a tank running down trees and bushes. Nothing like power to give a teenager delight! The saw blade to cut the railroad ties was about three feet around. The man who took care of the cutting had a lot of fingers missing. (Tough job!) My aunt would make me a sandwich with one large cut tomato, to fit between two pieces of white bread with lots of sugar spread on it. By lunchtime, the bread would melt from the daytime heat into the sugared tomato. (It was the greatest!) One time my cousin, Clyde, was taking a load of railroad ties to the lumberyard by truck. He asked me to go with him. Off we went, nearly killing a half dozen people when we arrived at the yard. The yardman told him to back the load into a particular area, my cousin said "hold on." He put the truck in reverse, stepped on the gas, burning rubber, and then hit the brakes hard. The front of the truck flew up into the air. I was looking to the sky when he stepped on the gas. The truck came down hard. The load was off in seconds and I thought that we were going to unload the truck by hand. (What a thrill.)

It was finally time for me to return to New York. My Uncle Doc liked the way I worked and asked me if I wanted to stay on the farm? He had already talked to my mother and father. They said it would be up to me. I said, "No!" It was so different on the farm. I guess I missed my little gang back in the city. I also knew that I would add to my uncle's family. That would have given my uncle one more acre of tobacco, according to the farming association. I must admit that I always wondered if that was the reason he asked me to stay?

Chapter 3: Back to New York

When I returned to New York, we had electricity, running water and a bathroom. I didn't know how good I had it! While I was gone, they opened night centers to keep the kids off the streets. This was one of the best things the Board of Education Department ever did. The Elks organized a basketball team, with my little gang and me. A great group, the Elks! When we won a game, they bought us banana splits at the local ice cream store. It was fun! That's when I felt I was finally good at something. My buddies looked up to me, so I worked harder to be better. We had a basket in the schoolyard. Even if I didn't have a ball, I would run and jump, trying to touch the rim until my legs gave out.

Me

B.P.O. ELKS No. 878 BASKETBALL - 1949-50

In junior high school, I was in a class that had some good basketball players. They helped me get even better before we got to the next level, high school.

TV

TV was starting to appear all over. It was something that was out of reach for our family, but my father, who was very mechanically inclined, invested most of his money in an RCA TV kit with a million pieces, which he put together with my brother. It took them weeks of soldering and reading plans. The whole family couldn't wait for the conclusion, but it finally came. We put the TV on top of a bookcase, which separated the dining room from the living room, with no cover on the TV. My brother plugged it in. We all stepped back while my father turned it on. All we got was a bright bar across the round 10-inch tube. Everyone's excitement dropped and we gave a big sigh. My father and brother went back to work for another couple of days. We were ready to try again. Everyone gathered around the TV, but not too close. We didn't trust it that much. My brother plugged it in. My father turned it on, and behold, a pattern appeared. We had TV! We then took out the two big bookcases that separated the two rooms, to make more room for the neighbors to sit. We watched Howdy Doody, Texaco Star Theater and wrestling. We even watched the pattern, when there was nothing on. It opened a new and exciting world. (Thanks, Dad!) I started thinking about girls and hair was starting to grow between my eyebrows. I also had this urge to go to a dance, which was at the local grammar school, PS 151. It was outside with lights and music. That's where our little gang would tease and holler at the dancers outside the fence until they called the cops. Now, I wanted to go, not letting the boys know about it. I guess it was that time. I even bought a pair of blue suede shoes. I knew how to dance, but I didn't think I had the nerve to ask a girl. We'll see. You had to wait in line to pay your 12 cents to get in. When one of the girls behind me said to the other girls that I was wearing eye makeup, they all started laughing! I just had to get out of there. Till this day, I can still feel that embarrassing moment. It was an ugly feeling for a young kid.

Sex

My best friend, Jacky, nicknamed Blimpy, was more advanced than me when it came to sex. One day at junior school, during recess outside, he walked up to each girl and said, "you want to get laid?" Finally, one girl said "yes!" Holy shit! Blimpy said, clearing his throat "well, we need another girl for my friend, Richie." She said "O.K." I'll bring my friend and we can meet in the schoolyard at 8 o'clock. I started thinking about my past embarrassment, and the feeling I had

21

was nervous, but stimulating. Eight p.m. finally came! I sat down on a bench with the other girl, putting my hand down her shirt with a little encouragement. Then she said, "lower." I couldn't find the damn thing! She had enough and decided to leave. The other girl was nude. Blimpy was masturbating, which I didn't know anything about! Blimpy's girl laid down on a turned over hockey net. She was ready for anything. I just wanted to see what it felt like to lay down on a nude girl without making a baby, for about 5 seconds. That's it! We left! The next morning, to my surprise, my left ball was swollen. My mother called Doctor Kriends and he came right over. After he examined me he said, "have you been near any girls lately?" I said, "no, not me!" He said, " if the swelling doesn't go down in a couple of days, I'll have to put a needle in it and draw out the infection." That scared the shit out of me! It finally went down. I stayed away from girls for a long time!

Bryant High School

Now I had to try out for the high school basketball team. Paul Courtois, the coach was an ex track champ in the Olympics and was looking for speed. Because of my shyness, my buddies from junior high school forced me to try out with them. The first thing the coach had us do was to line up against the gym wall and race to the other end. That's how I was picked. I was the fastest. I can still remember writing all kinds of things on my sneakers. Why, I didn't know. When I look at all the kids today with all the tattoos on their bodies, I believe it was the same thing.

During a game against our rival team, Long Island City High School, I was not aware that a girl had been stalking me. At the end of one of the games, the guys on my team said to me, "you have to go with us to Gildays," - a bar with a dance floor. I didn't drink and was afraid of girls. They told me that if I didn't go, this girl wouldn't go with us. They dragged me there! The girl's name was Jean. She got me up to dance and when I turned around the others had all gone. I was left alone with a girl by the name of Jean Preston. She lived in Astoria, Queens. We had to take the BMT L-train to get to her home. The temperature outside was in the 20's. I wasn't wearing clothes for those conditions, only a high school jacket and sneakers. It was cold, but it was a strange feeling, holding Jean to keep warm waiting for the train. Finally, the train came. We took it to Ditmars Blvd., the end of the line. Then we had to walk seven blocks. I was freezing! We walked up three flights, sat on the stairs and necked for an hour. I loved it and wasn't cold anymore. I had to see her again!

Discovering sex was like a drug. We would do it anywhere, under bushes, in the park, under the Boardwalk at Coney Island, and my left ball was okay! Before you knew it, she was pregnant! I had to tell the guys on the team. They were devastated! The team was just clicking together. I was just coming into my own on the basketball floor, scoring 27 and 36 points my last two games. It was a rotten feeling, like you just wanted to give up. Abortion was never talked about. That's when I found out what sympathy pregnancy was all about. (But of course we go on.)

Marriage # 1 (1951)

In 1951, my mother and father met Jean's family at our quick shotgun marriage. They were cordial with each other, that's all you could ask for. The only one who felt bad about the wedding was my youngest sister Barbara, who always thought we were going to get married. Jean got a job at John T. Stanley Soap Company and talked them into giving me a job in their factory. I needed to get my high school diploma to take advantage of a scholarship to Seton Hall University in New Jersey; given to me by their coach, Honey Russell. I was missing five majors, but was only allowed to take four per semester, so I went to the dean of boys who was the baseball coach, and told him of my problem. He went to the back room and eliminated one of my majors, which saved my having to go another semester. I started night school. Jean went with me to help. I got my diploma, with the best marks that I had ever received. I guess I just needed a push.

Coach Russell would have Jean and me come to Seton Hall and show us around, even invited to basketball games and sat behind the bench to see how the team and he worked. Things are looking good. But the inevitable happens. I had to go to work to support the family. I just couldn't take advantage of the scholarship.

Jean and I found a place to live in Weehawken, New Jersey, next to the Union Theater; the most famous of all strip joints. Nice neighborhood? Ha! The apartment was just on the other side of the Holland Tunnel. It was in the back of a house, over a garage, and roach infested. Pull the covers back and there they were! We saved our weekly paychecks under the mattress for the upcoming hospital bills. I didn't even realize that we were living a life of near squalor. As long as I had basketball to escape from my problems, I was happy, but I did wonder is this the life that is before me, or will I take another road that will lead me to a life of a better kind?

First Job

The brownstone building, where the soap factory was located, was on the lower west side of Manhattan, on the waterfront. It was just like a prison, with concrete floors and bars on the windows. Starting wages were $1.50 per hour. At the end of the day, I could just about walk. I was allowed a one-hour lunch and two fifteen minute breaks. My lunch, which consisted of 1 pint of chocolate milk and a jelly sandwich, held me for the day. The soap was made in big vats, cooled, cut up and packed into wooden crates. It was then shipped to South America. The job and conditions had to be the worst; summer with no air conditioning and winter without heat! This was my first job. What a way to start life!

I tried making friends with most of the guys who worked there, but most couldn't speak English. The foreman was a drunk Italian who didn't like me, for some reason or other. He probably didn't like anyone. The manager asked me if I would like the job of making the crates, with a bonus if I made over a certain amount. Yes! I could use the extra money. The bench that was used to put the boxes together made a quick and easy setup. I used a hammer with a hatchet at the other end that would cut the metal straps that held the bundles of wood, using one-penny nails to put the crates together. I would hammer over 4,000 one-penny nails a day, until they were backed up with more than enough crates. My right wrist had a knot on it, but it didn't keep me from taking a train into the city to play basketball in the evenings. Between my wrist and my feet, where the hell did I get all that energy? (Youth is a wonderful thing!)

Foreman

I had a close call when my foreman started cursing at me. I think he was pissed that I was making more money than he was, with my bonus. I couldn't take it any longer so I turned from making my boxes and told him to "shut up!" That really made him mad. He started coming at me with his hatchet raised, so I raised mine. I wanted him to know that I wasn't going to run. I also was standing on a bundle of wood, which kept my feet from hurting at my desk. This made me at least 6 inches taller than he was. He stopped on a dime in front of me and backed off. All the other workers cheered for me because they hated him. He didn't bother me after that. I wonder what would have happened if he hadn't stopped? (My life would have changed forever.)

Finally, A Break!

Jean and I moved to Astoria, Queens, thanks to Jean's mother and father. They got us an apartment next door to theirs. It was a three story walk-up that I remembered from the first night I met Jean. The apartment had a long hallway to a living room, small kitchen, bath and bedroom. It looked like a castle compared to the last place we lived.

Knowing now how I would look at my daughters' boyfriends, I know how Jean's mother and father looked at me when they met me for the first time. They were looking at a young boy who had no future, and didn't know anything about it, living one day at a time like most ignorant young kids. Now the mother and father were stuck with him.

Jean's father, Charlie, was a high-ranking V.F.W. (Veterans of Foreign Wars) official. He was put in the position of having to introduce us as husband and wife, to cover the pregnancy factor to all of his friends. He was an ill man. He suffered from tuberculosis from the war, and knew that the next time he went into the hospital he wouldn't come out alive. He was a good guy and even taught me to drive in a Henry J (that's one of the first American compact Ford cars). Finally that day came when he had to go into the hospital, but he rebelled and got into his car and headed out on Northern Boulevard, not knowing where he was going until he ran into a ditch. A call came to my in-laws apartment. It was a police officer asking my mother-in-law to come out and get him, but she couldn't, she was too overwrought. I borrowed a car and went. When I arrived, the officer was standing by the car in the ditch. He told me that he would have the car towed to a service station. I thanked him. I then picked up my father-in-law, like a baby, out of the driver's seat and took him to the nearest hospital where he died.

The funeral and all of the necessary happenings that went with it lasted for almost a week. All of the V.F.W. posts from all over the country wanted to pay their respects. It was heart breaking, especially for his wife. All the bands and the speeches at the funeral seemed to go on forever. Charley Preston was a great guy!

Birth

When it came time for the baby to be born, we rushed to the hospital and entered the lobby quickly moving to the counter where they wanted us to fill out some papers. That's when they found out that we were under age to sign a legal document, so they wouldn't let us in. A stranger in the lobby said he would sign us in. Thank God! A baby boy, Richard, Jr., was born and I was now a father.

Now we had to be careful so that we wouldn't have any more unexpected surprises, so I used condoms. One night, in a moment of passion, the condom broke. It was late. I panicked and ran out, trying to find a drug store to buy a douche, but all were closed. When I returned, we thought of using the baby's bath that had a drain in it. We filled it, putting a little vinegar in it. I submerged my face into it, blowing through the drain hose, which was then put into the correct location and I blew and blew, coming up for air periodically. Low and behold, it worked, after waiting for weeks. (The red river flows again) Boy that must have looked funny! (Do you think?)

Army Draft

I was reclassified from 1-A to 4-A after the baby was born, which means sole supporter and kept me out of the service. When my brother was drafted into the Army, one of the first things he did was to volunteer to be in the atom bomb test series called – "up shot knothole -- code -- Simon."

At the Nevada test site, he was in a trench 4000 yards from the blast. He even volunteered for the next test, but they wouldn't let him. That's my brother. I asked him to explain to me what it was like. He said he was lying down, looking up with his glasses on. When the blast went off, he could see jackrabbits shooting over his trench like bullets trying to get away from the inevitable concussion. When it hit, it was like you were in an alley during a hurricane. Later on in years, a lot of the men who were in these tests came down with all kinds of health problems. Not my brother. A story was done on him about how healthy he was. He eventually went on to do government work at Grumman on Long Island, New York, and worked on the first moon shot. He also started an ultra-light flying club in York, Pennsylvania, where he now  lives with his wife, Jean. He builds flintlock guns and is involved in reenacting the Civil War, in full dress. I'm so proud of my brother!

Back at Work

They finally fired me! The foreman turned me in to the

Union, the AFL-CIO, for working on my lunch hour. They said it made things difficult for the next guy who took my job to produce what I did. (That's a union for you!) I even had a job with Ashland House and Window Cleaning Company in downtown Wall Street, cleaning bathrooms and waxing floors on the midnight shift. Nothing was below me. I wasn't afraid of the future because I never thought about it.

Chapter 4: Finding Killeens - 1953

Around the corner from our apartment was a bar called Killeen's Tavern. Little did I know that it would be so big in my life. The following is taken from an article in Newsday, written by Lou Theodore, about how Killeen's was organized.

"During the early 1950's, prior to the massive TV sports agenda available today, Sunnyside Garden (located of course in Sunnyside, Queens) annually hosted an Open Basketball Tournament that featured all the great amateur stars of that era. The young teenagers who patronized Killeen's Tavern, located on 24th Street off Ditmars Boulevard in Astoria, regularly paid the one-dollar admission fee to see their basketball heroes perform. As if blessed by a magic wand, these same youngsters became basketball stars in their own right.

In late spring of 1955, they came to the conclusion that "hell, we can play with these guys!" And they were ever so right. They enlisted the help of one of their own with limited basketball ability, appointed him coach and directed him to field a team for the upcoming summer tournaments. The coach's name was Lou Theodore. When Theodore accepted the offer, the Killeen's Tavern dynasty was set in motion. Theodore persuaded Pat Kileen, owner of Killeen's Tavern, to sponsor the team and made the necessary arrangements to enter the team in the various tournaments. The Killeen's team was officially born.

All the pieces were put into place when Theodore started the recruiting process that would ultimately mold the team into a winner over the next dozen years.

The Killeen's crew drew packed houses whether playing at home, on the road, or at host tournaments like Rockville Center or Don Bosco. The team won championships in the Freeport Open (2), Rockville Center Open (5), Grenville Baker's Boys Club, (Locust Valley), Henry Street Pro Open and The Star Journal (3). They also provided entertainment against the pro house teams at hotels in the Catskills, and were one of the few (perhaps only) white teams to play in the Ruckers (Harlem) and the Ray Felix Open Tournaments (Corona) run by Cecil Watkins.

Most notable in this group of basketball stars were the charismatic and flamboyant Danny Doyle (he really is crazy) and the silver-haired Richie Bennett. Doyle was a fan favorite with his dunks, clowning around and horseplay; he, more than anyone, catered to the crowd at every opportunity. To the contrary, Bennett did his talking with tremendous speed, and a patented bank shot that many still discuss today."

I loved the article plus Danny and five others went on to the NBA.

Back to Killeen's

On Friday nights we would go into Manhattan and bounce around the city. We wouldn't have to wait in any lines, because we knew all the bouncers. They were mostly ex-ballplayers. Girls were plenty in number in those days. I remember meeting Don Ryan, a team mate of mine, in a bar. He was with a couple of girls. He introduced me to them and asked if I wanted a drink. I declined and said that I would rather go home and watch TV. One of the girls said, "me, too." She was thin, tall, and attractive. It was like she seized the opportunity to get laid. That's what we are looking for when we go to the city. Don, thinking fast, knowing I was married, gave me the key to his apartment. What a great guy! He had made other arrangements. Off we went to a night of pure sex! After the night was over, we grabbed a cab and dropped her off at the west side of Central Park. When I said "good night," she responded, "You don't want my phone number, right?" I said, "right." That's about how it was on a Friday night in the city. I wonder if I weren't married, where would that road with her have taken me?

Ski Trip

Another time, with the Killeen's gang, we all decided to take a ski trip to Mount Stowe, Vermont. We met in Astoria Queens and boarded a bus. On the way there, there was smoking and gambling. One of the guys opened the vent in the roof of the bus to let the smoke out. The bus driver stopped the bus and told us that he wasn't going any further until all the shit stopped. Big Dan said "O.K.! Get out of the bus and I'll drive." The driver had second thoughts and began to drive again. We finally arrived at the hotel. It was like a typical ski chateau, two levels with balconies all around. Real nice! We partied all night. The next morning, every one was at breakfast in a large dining room. The manager came in with two state troopers. He then started pointing out certain people in our group and saying in his German accent, "I want him out, and him and him." At that moment, Big Dan got up out of his seat and announced, "everyone go up to your room and flush a towel down the toilet." The whole group started getting up like robots at Danny's command. The manager hesitated, realizing he was caught in a no win situation. He blurted out, "Wait a minute," in his German accent. "Let's talk." So the manager and the state troopers, Dan and Don Ryan made a deal. The two state troopers would escort us for the next two days. It's great to be young!

Race Track

Another time, Lou, the coach of Killeen's, had a Trotter running at Yonkers Raceway. He invited all the Killeen' boys to go, because the race was supposed to be fixed. He said it was the third race and told us to put all our money on his horse and we did tentatively. Sure as hell, the horse came in

32

first at 17 to 1. We collected the winnings, but if only we had believed, we would have bet our shirts. That's always the afterthought.

While we were collecting the money, one of the guys from another team that we played a couple of weeks earlier, came up to us and said to me, "you still have black eyes?" That's because I had a fight with one of his teammates in Elmhurst, an all black area that we played for the championship, and won. At the end of the game a fight broke out. I was on the floor after I threw the first punch. Everyone piled on top of me. The guys were kicking me. The girls were trying to pull the eyeballs out of my sockets until two players from the other team pulled me out of there. Most of the time, when I started a fight, I could get one punch in, and then my teammates would come in behind me. This time it didn't work.

Following a lot of our games, Lou, our coach and Professor at Manhattan College, would get sororities to throw us parties. How good could life be? My marriage was getting weaker. I'm finding out that I'm missing out on a lot. Getting married so young is the worst thing you can do!

Chapter 5: Moving Up In Life! - 1956

One of my basketball friends told me that the First National City Bank of New York would give me a job just to play ball for them. They had many great ball players on their team, from colleges in New York and even some ex-pros. We played together well and were undefeated. The Bank's officials just loved beating all the other Banks.   While I would sit at my desk, the V.P.'s would come in and talk about the games with me. The poor guys sitting at the desks behind me were unnoticed. They had been there all of their working lives, but no one noticed them. (Strange life we live.) One day, a couple of my team mates were called into the office and were told that they had a choice, to quit the bank or be fired. They were caught shaving points back in college. I really felt bad for them because they wanted to make a career in the banking business. (But you've got to pay your dues!)

The main office of the F.N.C.B. was located on Wall Street, a totally different life than I was used to. All the other guys would go down to the local Wall Street haberdashery and have their suits made. I bought my suits from Robert Hall, you know, the "plain pipe racks" store. I finally gave in and had one made too. It made me feel good. Little did I know that some day I would be wearing suits in Gentlemen's Quarterly magazine? Now I'm really starting to feel I'm missing out on a lot in life, which is taking more of a toll on my marriage. The bank life was a big step moving up in life for me. It was more like life should be, in comparison to where I was coming from. Our bank team traveled to Chicago, to play the F.N.C.B. of Chicago. They took us out the night before the game to a nightclub called the Chez Perez, where we saw Edie Gorme and Steve Lawrence. I had a little too much to drink. I never could drink! I even had enough nerve to go back stage and get Edie's autograph. I had no way of knowing that the Chez Perez would later come back into my life, as well as Chicago.

The next day we played the game. I fouled out quickly and we lost. The coach blamed me. He was right! I stunk! That night we partied hard, trying to forget the loss. I remember throwing my shirt out the window of the hotel where I stayed because I didn't want my wife to see it. The shirt was full of lipstick stains. (Chicago was a wild town.)

Drag Strip
When I returned from Chicago, Jean (my wife), and I thought we had enough money coming in to purchase a used

34

'54 Olds 88 car. For entertainment we would go watch the drag races at the unfinished Brooklyn Queens Expressway just off the Triborough Bridge. It had about a quarter mile straight run with 25-foot high walls on each side. It became one of the hottest drag strips in Queens. We watched from on top of the wall with hundreds of other fans. I thought I would give it a try. When my chance came I lined up against a 1957 Chevy. I was very nervous, but all I had to do was just step on the gas. It was an automatic, so no problem. I can still remember the feeling in the pit of my stomach. At the starting line the other driver looked over at me and revved his engine. It sounded tough, so I revved my powerful Olds 88 engine. We were ready. I was going to run this guy off the road! The starting flag went down. We burned rubber. I was staying with the Chevy, my hands were tight on the wheel, pushing the gas pedal through the floor, trying to find more speed. The Olds shifted into second gear. That's when I couldn't believe my eyes; the Chevy started pulling away like I was standing still, totally embarrassed. I couldn't resist pulling up alongside of the Chevy after the race and asking what he had under the hood. He answered, "it was something new, they call it fuel injection," ending my racing career.

Brooklyn Tournament

There was a basketball tournament in Brooklyn, N.Y. that the guys from the bank asked me to play in, outside the Bank League. I said that I would. What I didn't know was that a team that I played with in Queens, N.Y., was in the same tournament. And wouldn't you know it? We ended up playing against each other in the final game. We were favored by 6 points. I was having a good game so they put Dom Debonis on me, one of the better defensive players, (they called him the animal). He was ahead of me at Bryant High School. I loved the way he played. He ended up being the captain of the N.Y.U basketball team, and was my idol! That didn't stop him from putting me into the wall. As I faked a jumper and tried to drive around him, my first response was to get up and go at him; but Mike Parente, 6'9", got in between us, holding us apart with his two arms standing against a wall. That's when Ted Rickter, from the other team, hit Mike with a right, snapping his head back into the wall, causing a 3 inch gash to the back of his head. We were stunned! It was a sucker punch. I can still see Mike holding the back of his head and saying to Ted, "Nice going, Ted!" They took Mike to the hospital and the game went on.

We were up by 5 points, with 30 seconds to go. The other team froze the ball. They lost the game, but beat the spread and collected thousands of dollars. (That's N.Y. for you!) After the game, we all went to a local bar where I told Dom Debonis that he always was my idol in high school. At that moment, he proceeded to hug and kiss me like any real Italian would do. After that, no one would dare rough me up while Dom was around. We became great friends and it was a good thing that Mike had stopped me from going at Dom because he would have killed me.

There was one game I will never forget. It was with Dan Palmer's social club team that had a winning streak of 55 games. We were playing another game just like any other, except for a tragic ending. There were two brothers on the opposing team, Ed and John. I was guarding John, who was having one of the best shooting games I have ever seen. The gym was packed standing room only. John's family was also there rooting him on and his team was up six points in the fourth quarter, with minutes to go. Then the tragedy happened. John's father got so excited that he had a massive heart attack and died on the spot. It put a stop to the game. They were awarded the win, but at a high price.

Sands Resort

Dick Crosby, a basketball friend of mine, told me that the Sands Resort on Long Island would give me a cabana and a membership to the club, if I would play in an exhibition game every Sunday for them. Now that I had a car, I agreed to do it. Dick played for the Washington Generals against the Globetrotters and knew a lot of tricks to entertain the crowd. One was, he would guard me closely as I came close to the foul line for a jump shot, he would grab my legs as I was going up, and he would throw me up. The crowd gasped at the height of the jump, but the hardest part was coming down. I never made the shot, but it was fun and I felt good about belonging to a club. The Sands had a massive amount of young girls. They were my cheering section and invitations were abundant. Dick was also a car dealer and offered me a job as a salesman. I turned him down because I still had a problem with dyslexia, which kept me from doing a lot of things that would have helped me in life.

Kidnapped

St. Anthony's, a team in South Manhattan, where a basketball tournament was being held they asked me to play with them, offering me some good money. I felt I could squeeze it in before a 9 PM game in Queens, with Killeen's that same night. They told me to meet them at 5 PM at their clubhouse in the village, to get ready for a 6 PM tip off; which I did. At the clubhouse everything seamed to be moving in slow motion and no one was even talking to me. I began getting nervous because my wife, Jean, was to meet me at the 9 o'clock game. I finally realized that it was all a big act. In reality, I was being kidnapped. It was a perfect acting job by the St. Anthony's team. They knew that I couldn't make the 9 o'clock game, so they put the show on. We (St. Anthony's) won the game, and found out as I was leaving the gym that Killeen's won the 9 PM game in Queens also, without me. (That's' the real basketball world.)

WHY?

Coming from a basketball workout in the city, I headed back to Queens by train, from the Lexington Avenue station. This time, paid my way through the turnstile, without flattening out a penny. I started to go down the stairs that led to the platform, when a man ran up passing me hollering, "Man on the tracks, man on the tracks." From the top of the stairs I could see everyone looking toward the other end of the station. The people were three and four deep. For some reason, I started running, pushing my way through the crowd. It was like I had no control of myself, no thought except getting to this person. Halfway there, instead of fighting the crowd, I jumped down onto the tracks, running to this person who I could visibly see now laying on the tracks. No consideration was given to the possibility of a train coming. I finally got to him; an older man, about 225 pounds, wearing an overcoat with a cut on his forehead. I tried to lift him. It was impossible by myself. I looked up at all the people watching me struggling. I hollered angrily up to them, "Give me a hand." (In a nice way, ha!) At last one man jumped down, then a second, then a third, not caring about the possibility of danger. We lifted the man up. The people on the platform put their hands down and helped pull us up. Just then my train came in on the other side. I quickly boarded it, leaving the scene, not even knowing if the man was dead or alive.

I sat down, exhausted, trying to figure out what exactly had happened, when a lady seated across from me said,

"There should be more men like you!" It's probably the last time a woman would say that to me! Embarrassed, I acknowledged her, not looking into her face, I put my head back and started thinking "why?" People jump into freezing rivers, burning buildings and don't know why, it seems, when something dramatic happens you don't have time to think, you dive right into it, like the people standing on the train platform when the man fell on the tracks. They just looked. At least one man ran for help, but the others must have thought it to be too dangerous or thought about family, so the impulse to jump into the situation was gone. That's my point of view. So New Yorkers aren't so bad. They just need a little encouragement. (What makes us tick?)

Chapter 6: How I Got Started In Modeling

On Friday nights all the guys would go bar hopping. I guess it's the excitement of what the night would bring. It must be the animal instinct in us. We ended up in a bar on about 61st and 3rd Ave when this guy came up to me and asked if I ever modeled? I said, "No!" At first everyone was a little leery of this guy, until he gave me his card, which looked legitimate. He asked me to come to his office on Monday to try some clothes on for a job. With encouragement from the guys, I told him that I would. Well, here we go! This started me on a new road. (Which was like a dream.)

I arrived at the office. It was first class. The clothes fit right off the rack. They love that! It meant I was the right size, 40 Regular, and 6' tall. The job was for Gentlemen's Quarterly magazine. They told me to get an agent. They suggested the Burke, McHugh Agency to get started, so I went. I was going to be in an environment that I didn't know, so I was a little nervous.

I walked into their office. Everybody was good-looking and well dressed. I was afraid to make friends with anyone because I thought that they were all weird and they seemed to be acting all the time. Where is the real person?

I was sent to get some test shots, which means that a photographer took pictures of you at no cost, giving both of us pictures. They started me out with $45 an hour. I did get the job with G. Q. Magazine, a full-page shot (on right). It was a great feeling, but I wouldn't let anyone know it. There were other things to do, like walking all over the city, giving out my

composites. That is, two pages of the best pictures from your portfolio. Most of the photographers who looked at the pictures told me that they were amateurish. I think they said that only because they hadn't taken them! One photographer in the Village area showed me a composite that was given to him by Grace Kelly, so she made the rounds also. (Interesting)

There was another job with GQ. I was getting ready in

the dressing area, waiting for the photographers to set up for a raincoat ad, when this girl model came up to me and asked if I would tighten a scarf that was wrapped around her chest? It was to flatten her breasts. I started tying the knot and asking her if it was too tight? I was thinking what a great job this was. Another modeling job was shot for a cover of a record album. It was on location in the city in an alleyway and the weather was in the 20°'s. We were on our 10th take, meaning we were outside for a long time, when a gentleman who owned one of the apartments came out and invited all of us into his home for coffee and to warm-up. The man's name was Mitch Miller who had his own TV show called "Sing Along with Mitch". He was big at that time. People aren't so bad in New York City.

The Cruise

I found that I love this modeling world. You never know what kind of a job is coming next, like doing a brochure for the home line on a ship called the Italia. It had seven nightclubs. I got to dress up and drink champagne every night with four beautiful models for two weeks over New Year's. This was to Nassau and Haiti. I was also treated like a celebrity, and had

the neatest cabin, and was even involved in the show on board ship. I remember coming on board and two women approached me wearing their expensive fur coats. They invited me to a pajama party, where the men would wear the tops and women would wear the bottoms. I didn't go, but it must have been a wild party. The first thing that we did on board ship was to go to the pool and show off our bodies. But it didn't take long for one of the girls to come down with sun poisoning. That put her out for the rest of the trip,

so we all moved away from the pool thing. What a way to learn. When we stopped at Haiti, I decided to take a bike ride up the mountain and take some pictures. I wanted to see how the other half of this place lives. While riding by an old lady in a grass hut, I snapped her picture. Little did I know that I had just stolen her soul, she began chasing me, throwing rocks and hollering. I wish someone had told me about these quirky people. Back to the ship to get ready for New Year's Eve, while preparing, my voice started changing and turning into laryngitis. That's going to make it very difficult for me to communicate with my dancing partners, whom I found I couldn't manipulate into bed without a voice. Live and learn. The Italian band kept playing the hit song, Volare over and over again. It was driving me nuts.

I became good friends with the star of the show, a magician by the name of Jack London. He could tell you the card in your hand without even touching the deck. Now my big time came when I was on stage and had to tie Jack in a straitjacket. I thought I was doing well until Jack told me, in a whisper, to put my knee in his back and tie it tight. So I did, thinking to myself, did I make it too tight? With very little effort he got out with no problem. The guy was amazing. When returning to New York. We all took advantage of the low prices on Joy perfume and Rum. We all took our limit home. I just can't believe I got paid for this job.

Hercules Unchained

The modeling agency that I was with, received passes to parties. One was to the opening of "Hercules Unchained," a movie that Steve Reeves starred in. The party was held at Rockefeller Center. Steve didn't make the party because of tax problems. If he came to the United States; they would've nailed him to the wall. The party went on without him. All we had to do was to circulate around and look like someone. I was enjoying looking at all the Italian beauties. I have never seen so many busts exposed. They look like hams being served on a platter! They must have had some extra support to hold them up. Playboy had nothing over these girls. I got to meet Robert Young, who was a big star then on TV in the sit-com, "Father Knows Best." I didn't know what he was doing at the party, but he was enjoying himself. I tried to communicate with some of the beauties there, but they have themselves on such a high pedestal that you felt like nothing in comparison to them. I guess that put me in my place.

I loved seeing my pictures in magazines and ads. It made me feel important. I was hoping that my friends and family might be impressed and think that I was doing very well in the business, but that's youth.

Gloria Swanson

Then I was sent to a client by the name of Gino, who was in from Italy. He was getting ready to do a fashion show at the New York Athletic Club, featuring Italian style clothes versus the American styles. Gino selected me to wear his clothing line. All the media, newsreels and celebrities were there. This was a lot bigger than I thought. I was very nervous. I had never walked out on a runway in my life and it seemed like the whole world was out there. On the runway, one of the outfits I wore had pants with high pockets. I wore a sweater that covered the pockets. When I got to the end of the runway, someone yelled out, "let's see the pockets." I didn't do it like a professional. I lifted the sweater up with my two hands and everyone laughed. I wasn't kidding around, but they thought I was. The final result was they picked one of the suits I wore to be used for a motion picture. Gloria Swanson had some pictures taken with me and she was very angry because she wasn't wearing the right makeup. I wondered how many kinds there are? It was in all the Newsreels the next day. I'm feeling pretty good now.

I was at a table after the show with Gino and others, soaking up all the attention I was getting, when a gentleman came over and said to me, "Miss Swanson would like you to join her at her table." I said, "okay," but never got to go. I just couldn't get away. Today, I feel bad about that.

Gino had rented a large house upstate where he threw a big party after the show. There were rose bushes all over the place. He asked me to stay overnight. I accepted. The party went well. They had spaghetti as the main course and of course we needed cheese. I said that I would get it. I went into the kitchen and saw the grated cheese on the counter. I took it back. The first person to use it found it was grated soap! That was so bad! When the party was over, I was in my room getting ready for the night when Gino came in. Yes! He was making a move on me. I acted like I didn't understand what he was talking about and he backed off. I found out later that in the modeling business; the clients and photographers were the ones you had to watch out for, rather than the models. The guys on my basketball team kidded me that they wouldn't take a shower with me!

A Different Kind of Model

I did a test shooting with a new female, an aspiring model named Daphne. I started seeing her and then found out she was a high priced prostitute. I guess modeling covered her other income. I wanted to ask her more about what and how she got started. (But no.) I chickened out. I'll just leave well enough alone.

We met as much as possible. I think she wanted someone outside of her world. I invited her to a Killeen's basketball game, to be played in Brooklyn outside at night under the lights. We were running late when I picked her up. The team was warming up when we arrived. I dropped her off and ran into the locker room for a quick change. When I came out, there were some guys warning everyone that I was coming. Everyone cheered when I came onto the court. I looked up and there was a dummy of me, hanging from a lamppost. It seems the week before I had a fight with one of the local stars. We knocked them out of the tournament. This was their way of getting back at me. They burned me in effigy at half time. What a weird experience! We were playing against St. John stars when I had a fight with Leroy Elles, a 7 foot black guy who went on to play with the L.A. Lakers. This was Daphne's introduction to my world. (She didn't like it!)

Our relationship was growing weaker. I don't know who was taking advantage of whom; there were still certain things we didn't talk about like her profession and the future. When I called her the last time, she said she had to go shopping with her mother, which was the first time she didn't respond to my call. I decided that was her way of telling me that it finally came to an end. Most relationships end like that.

Chapter 7: New York Knicks Basketball

When I was playing amateur ball, I really loved it because I was in a comfort zone, plus other players looked up to me. I looked forward to playing it for the rest of my life. I never thought that I would ever get the opportunity of playing in the NBA. You never know where the road of life is going to take you. One day I received a card in the mail that said, "a squad of players and aspirants of the New York Knickerbockers Pro basketball team will practice in the Holy Family gymnasium in Brooklyn, starting on Tuesday the ninth at 7 p.m.. The group will work out under the direction of Fuzzy Lavan, head coach, and Red Holtzman, assistant coach. You are cordially invited to attend these practices. They will be held September 9, 10, 11, and 12, and also September 16, 17, 18 and 19. All practices start at 7 p.m." I was excited, but this was only a workout, I thought. Then it dawned on me that I was actually getting a chance to make the team.

After thinking about it, I had the feeling that I could play with the pros. This was because I had played with Dick McGuire, captain of the New York Knicks, and his brother Al the sport's announcer. Dick and Al would tend bar at his family's restaurant at 108th St. Rockaway Beach, Queens, New York. I would look for every opportunity to

108th Street Rockaway Beach

play with and against them. A lot of the pros from the NBA would come to play and to spend time with Dick and Al. That's when I knew I could play with the pros. Dick had a book on me. It was for telling how to play defense on another player. It was loose on top and tight in the corners. That's because I had a bank shot from the corner, that I rarely missed. (See picture of me dunking --->)

I believe I got this chance to try out because of an All-Star game that I had played. It was the New York All-Stars against the Long Island All-Stars; mainly college players. The New York coach asked me to join their team, which was run by an ex-New York Knick, Ray Lump. There were other New York Knick players there, putting on clinics. Pro-scouts were also there. My cousin, Don Hill, and his father came to see the game. Don held the scoring record at Queens College for a long time, so he was very interested in the game.

At half time I went over to Don and his father. We were losing, and I had scored only two points. They asked me what's wrong? I told them, "no problem, we'll get them the second half," hoping and praying to myself that we would. Lo and behold, at the end of the game, I had scored 22 points. We won the game, and I received the MVP award. I think that and other tournaments around New York against top college players led to this tryout. If one made it through these practices, they would be invited to the Knicks training camp.

I met two players who I played against in the CYO league. They were Pete Brennan and Joe Quigg. They played for the University of North Carolina and went undefeated in the past year and now were going for the gold. I arrived here the sloppy way. But here we are. At one of the workouts Pete Brennan came up to me. He was about 6' 6". He told me his sister says "hello". I gulped. Then he said, "You met her at Rockaway Beach." Now I remembered. She was beautiful and reminded me of Daisy May. I was barhopping with a friend of mine, Wally DiMasi, when this Daisy May walked by. I had a few drinks, which gave me courage to chase her down the street, pleading with her to have a drink with me. She finally agreed. We had a great time talking basketball. She did tell me that her brother played, which I took with a grain of salt, not knowing he was a star at North Carolina University. After a few drinks, we retreated to my car and necked for a while. I was still married to Jean, so there was no future for us, but I was glad she remembered me. It's a small world. I said to Pete, please say hello to her for me, and I walked away slowly.

I played well all through the practices. Red Holtzman liked me, which gave me courage to keep working hard. After the tryouts I was depressed because I felt that I probably didn't make it. I'm just a high school kid who shouldn't be here anyway. Just waiting for the decision was frustrating. Finally, I was contacted and was told that I had made the team. At that moment, I had a good chill running through my body. It was a great feeling of accomplishment. How did I get this far? Now I'm on my way to Greenwich, Connecticut to get a shot at

the big time and have to go through this all over again (oh boy).

The First National City Bank was excited for me and gladly gave me a leave of absence to pursue this experience. The camp was set up in Greenwich, Connecticut. We stayed at the old Greenwich Inn, a beautiful place located in one of the most exclusive areas of Connecticut with all you could eat of the very best foods. Workouts were two times a day, six days a week, plus six exhibition games, four with the Syracuse Nationals and two with Philadelphia. During one of the workouts I tore the side of my sneaker. The Knicks gave us two pair of Keds, but I only liked Converse, Chuck Taylor low-cuts. I felt I had more freedom and didn't like my ankles wrapped, so I was allowed to go to New York to pick up a new pair. That gave me a chance to go home and see my wife during that time. Jean took a picture of me in my Knicks uniform that I had brought home to show her. She was so happy for me that I was doing something that I loved. That started to give me a complex about my cheating on her. I wanted to tell her and get it off my mind. I guess the lure of the outside world finally got to me. I finally opened up and told her. She didn't say anything for a moment and then said, "let's talk about it when you get back from Camp." I thought that was a good idea and just wanted to get out of there. (I felt shitty.)

My roommate was Willie Naulis from UCLA, one of the few blacks on the Knicks. At that time, he was a great guy and had a great record collection. When we had time, we would drive around Greenwich, Connecticut looking at the lodge homes and talking about all the problems that were going on at that time around the country. At our apartment, if one of my girlfriends called and I wasn't there, he would keep her on the phone for long periods of time talking about what, I don't know. He was real cool.

The Knicks had plenty of personality problems. There were fights. One of the big rookies irritated Richie Guerin. He was really trying to control himself until the rookie pushed him too far. Richie got him in a headlock, pulled him down to the ground and kept hollering at him. Are you going to leave me alone? After that Richie had no more problems with him. He was a man after my own heart. Richie was one of the stars on the Knicks. He would help me run through plays telling me to cut right and left, which he didn't have to do. I'm sorry I didn't get to know him better. About conditioning, we were told not to lift weights or swim in cold pools. What a difference compared to today's sports thinking and conditioning. Most of the guys were distant from each other. I was the worst. I don't know why. I'll have to check with my psychiatrist. Having my car helped me a lot to get around. We all decided to go out to dinner. Ray Felix, a 7-foot center on the team, was standing outside the inn waiting for us, when we came out the door. He started jumping up and down like a wild Indian. He didn't realize he was standing on a fire ant hill. We couldn't stop laughing. You just have to picture that. When we finally got into my car, Ray had to sit in the passenger seat with his head bent over, so it wouldn't hit the ceiling. It was a very uncomfortable looking sight. I guess that's why he only had convertibles. This is what big men have to put up with. As far as the coaching went, I always felt that they didn't include the bench enough in the starting five workouts. Consequently, when we were put in we really didn't know what he wanted. When I was put in, I did my own thing, which was to run. The papers even wrote that I had a way of speeding the game up. I worked with Red Holtzman most of the time. I liked him. We got along great. The Knicks had a nickname for me. They called me Peter Pan because I was always flying all over the place.

Curfew

We would break the 11 p.m. curfew most every night. Girls would invite the whole team to their homes to party. At one party I was in my car with a girl. I will never forget what she said to me quote, "These guys think we put out for everybody, but you're different". I thought to myself, I'm in now. All of a sudden there was a knock on the steamed up windows of the car. One of the guys said let's get out of here, one of the girls just cut her wrist. They piled in the car and off we went back to the inn. The next day we got word that she was okay. Richie Guerin collected money from each of us to buy her a watch. I guess to cover the scar. It didn't get into the papers. If it were today, it would have been all over the news. Of course, the coach heard about it, which led to a meeting the next night. Vince Barila, an ex-New York Knickerbocker player, was the main speaker. He made it very clear that the next time someone broke the curfew, no matter who they were, they would be thrown off the team. (It worked.)

Cutting the players as we progressed was pretty quick. One player from the Eastern league, who was averaging 40 points a game there, was one of the first to be cut. The other rookies were on edge thinking that they were the next to be cut. Camp was a different world. It wasn't the same as amateur ball. We were fighting for a job. It was sad in a way. I had no pressure. I felt like an outsider looking in.

My first game was against the Syracuse Nationals in New Jersey. When I was called on to get into the game, I was nervous. I felt like my legs were moving too fast. I finally settled down, scored a layup and two jumpers for six points. This wasn't too bad for a start. There were some of my old teammates at the game. At halftime they told me that I was going to make the team, but I felt differently. At another game in Long Island, my mother and father went along with my uncle and cousins to see me play. It was the only game my father ever saw and it was my mother's second. Who says you need family to push you to heights? My mother always thought I was going to have a heart attack when she saw me play once in high school. At the Knicks game in the first half I took a jump shot from the foul line. It hit the back of the rim and bounced high. Tiry, the Knicks center, hit the ball back to me. I went up again, this time I made it. In the second half, I was going down on a fast break, ahead of the field. I took a big step. I was going to dunk it in front of my mother and father and show off to the crowd. That big step gave someone behind me a chance to catch up to me and put the ball down my throat with an elbow to my head. I was feeling for blood that wasn't there, pleading to the referee that I was fouled, to no avail. Live and learn. The Knicks also put on clinics at the local high schools, teaching the fundamentals of basketball. At the end of the program, Felix, Tiry and Sears, the three big seven footers, would dunk the ball, then I would go last and the announcer introduced me as the fastest man in the NBA. I loved that! Then I would attempt to dunk and close out the show. When you dunk the ball in basketball, you hang in the air. They call that hang time. It would leave such an impression on me that I would dream at night that I would jump and hang in the air and not come down. I would even start to rise. It's the greatest feeling, defying gravity.

Levane Delays Final Cuts Until After All-Star Game

BY MURRAY JANOFF

The Knicks' 121-116 loss to Syracuse at Wantagh High School Saturday night caused Coach Fuzzy Levane to withhold planned cutting of the squad. He wants more time to be sure of keeping the right players.

The rookie crop hasn't produced any eye-opening prospects thus far. Matter of fact, one of the key newcomers, North Carolina's Joe Quigg of Levittown, hasn't worked out in the exhibitions and was placed on the disabled list for an indefinite period.

Quigg, who is still strengthening his leg which was broken last year, is returning to North Carolina where he'll assist Coach Frank McGuire and possibly take additional studies in the spring semester.

HE'S THE THIRD player the Knicks have lost officially this season. The first two were Mel Hutchins, the veteran all-star who quit because of a knee that won't heal properly, and Johnny Lee, the Yale star who returned to school for post graduate work, passing up the professional game.

Levane had intended cutting his current 14-man squad by one, and possibly two players, but after Saturday's game, he said:

"I've got to wait now a few more days, possibly until after Tuesday's game with Philadelphia (in Poughkeepsie) or even as long as after the game with the College All Stars Saturday night (in the Garden). I want to be as sure as possible before I make the cuts."

Saturday night's game, for the benefit of the Wantagh School's Scholarship Fund, was the second in two nights and the third overall between the two teams. The Nats beat the Knicks, 2-1, but neither team is concerned over the actual scoring outcome. They are cooperative in giving each other's rookies a workout. For example, the Nats started a veteran five against the Knick rookies on Friday night. The Knicks returned the favor on Saturday night.

THE GAME provided a feeling that the Nats got more help in the rookie draft than did the Knicks. About the Knick newcomers . . . Mike Farmer of San Francisco didn't play much because of blisters on his feet . . . Pete Brennan from North Carolina missed on his jump-shot too many times . . . Jerry Bird from Kentucky showed drive but poor defense . . . Dick Bennett from Astoria displayed plenty of speed and a fair jump shot, but missed defensive assignments also.

The Nats are down to 11 players, including Seymour, who will again be player-coach.

He'll have to chop one, but not until Dec. 1. His three rookies showed plenty. Big Connie Dierking from Valley Stream has a potent hook shot. Hal Greer is fast, a good shooter and fairly clever. Little Tommy Kearns is another speedster, but may have to overcome a size deficiency. He's only about 5-9.

Knicks (116)				Syracuse (121)			
Braun	0	9	18	Schayes	4	8	16
Bird	0	0	0	Palazzi	0	2	2
Gallo	0	1	1	Conlin	0	0	0
Sobie	0	0	0	Hopkins	3	2	8
Felix	9	3	21	Dierking	9	2	20
Tyra	6	8	20	Kerr	3	1	7
McCann	0	0	0	Bialotto	5	2	12
Brennan	2	4	8	Bianco	0	0	0
Bird	0	0	0	Greer	0	0	0
Brennan	0	1	1	Kearns	9	13	31
Farmer	0	0	0				
Totals	43	30	116	Totals	47	27	121

53

Cut from The Knicks

One of the assistant coaches was a friend of mine and would let me know what went on at all the coaches' meetings. He told me that Red Holtzman didn't want to let me go, but on the way from a Philadelphia game by bus; Fuzzy Levane the head coach gave me the news that I had been cut from the team. In a way I felt relieved. They sent me to play for a new team, the Allentown Jets in the Eastern League in Pennsylvania. I had to earn it by trying for a spot on the team. It went like this. I played basketball with a lot of black ballplayers. I had some favorites like Vernon Stokes, who deserved the nickname, "The General." He was an ex-St. Francis star who didn't get a chance in the big time. Another was Stacy Arsenault, a great ballplayer, and a good friend. George Fox was very close. We worked and played together at the bank. I even introduced George to his wife, whom I'd met at the bank. She worked in another section and was beautiful. I told George he had to meet her, so I arranged it. It worked and before you knew it, they were married. I felt good about that!

That one spot that was open on the Jets team, would you believe it, was between George and me. It's funny, you come all this way, to be knocking one of your friends out of something that they love, but that's how life goes. Finally the decision was made. They picked me. When it was all over, George said to me, "they picked you because you're white". I was crushed. But maybe he was right. Life goes on.

The Jets started out paying me $35 a game. The Knicks said that they would keep an eye on me. The Eastern League is made up of many small towns in Pennsylvania. Most games were played on weekends so that the players could hold jobs during the week. They also let in players who were caught shaving points in college. We stayed in old hotels and traveled on snowy and icy roads. Things were bad. Playing ball was like playing in high school. Whoever got the ball first, shot it. Not much teamwork.

ALLENTOWN JETS
Front row: Dick Bennett, Capt. Jerry Paulson, George Fox, Tom Hart, Sonny Hill.
Stand.: George Conrad, Bill Katheder, Kurt Englebert, Jim Tucker, Art Spolestra.

THE HOME TEAM

CAPT. JERRY PAULSON — A fine backcourtman with 'radar' in his jump shot. Won All-Metropolitan honors as a member of the Manhattan College team two years ago. Broke into pro ball with the Cincinnati Royals. Played last year with the Wilmington Jets and averaged 22 points per game. Held in very high regard throughout the league.

BILL 'SONNY' HILL — At 5 ft., 9 in. one of the few little men in the league. Because of his extraordinary jumping ability can easily be called the 'biggest little man in basketball'. Can dunk the ball from a standing position. Smooth floorman and also possesses a deadly outside jump shot.

KURT ENGLEBERT — 6 ft., 5 in. St. Joseph's College grad. Got his start with the Jets in Wilmington last year after being drafted

the Syracuse Nationals in the NBA. Spent last year on tour with the 'Goose' Totum All Stars. His 6 ft., 6 in. help on the inside and he drives well off Coach McCann's offense.

BILL KATHEDER — 6 ft., 6 in. former LaSalle College standout. Moves well for a big boy and appears ready to make the transition from college to pro ball which many men can never make. Good defensive man and can score from inside or out with good variety of shots. Particulary good set shot.

DICK BENNETT — Classy New York City boy with no college experience. Came to the Jets from the New York Knickerbockers. Coach 'Fuzzy' LeVane of the Knicks rates him very highly. A smooth playmaker and good shot with tremendous speed.

DICK BENNETT — Classy New York City boy with no college experience. Came to the Jets from the New York Knickerbockers. Coach 'Fuzzy' LeVane of the Knicks rates him very highly. A smooth playmaker and good shot with tremendous speed.

Divorce # 1 (1960)

My divorce, after seven years of marriage, finally was over. I left with my clothes and trophies. The girl I was going with, whom I'd met at the bank, Vicky, lived in Forest Hills Queens and felt I needed transportation since I lost my car in my divorce. She bought me a car - a 1951 MG TD. To celebrate, we went to Belmar, New Jersey on the shore for a couple of days to get away from it all in a quiet little town. The first bar we went into the bartender knew me. He said there was a party that night and would we like to come? So much for a quiet little town. When I returned to my apartment in Queens, that I rented by the week, I called my agency, to see if there were any calls for me. They told me: "There is some mail there for you". When I retrieved it, one was from Playboy Magazine, which I thought was for a subscription, but when I opened it, it was Playboy asking me to come to Chicago for a shooting. I called to make sure it wasn't a joke. They said

they were expecting me. Holy shit! That's all I have to say. I checked the oil and I packed up the car and said goodbye to all my friends on my way out of town, so I couldn't be stopped.

When I called Vicky to say that I was on the road and headed for Chicago, she responded by telling me that she was pregnant. I knew she wasn't and I went on. This was bad. I even kept the car. Nobody's perfect. I drove along with the theme song playing from Midnight Cowboy. I sang the words, "Everybody's talking at me, I don't hear a word they're saying." I kept going.

Chapter 8: Playboy - Arriving In Chicago

The night before my appointment with Playboy, I could hardly sleep, thinking about what I was going to do and why they picked me. The Playboy offices were located in the old Chez Paree building. When I arrived there, I gave my name to the receptionist, hoping that she would know who I was. She did. What a relief. She showed me to a room to try some clothes on for the shot. The people were just great. I was treated like a special person that made me feel more at ease with everyone gathered around me, straightening my shirt and getting the lights just right. When a gentleman came into the room, everyone separated, letting him walk up to me. He said, "Richard Bennett, I'm Hugh Hefner. It's a pleasure to have you with us." He impressed me and everyone liked him and of course I knew he was Hef. The shot was for a story about a girl whose face they projected onto my shirt. As you can see, that gave it an eerie shadow effect. The smoke from the cigarette was killing my right eye, but that's show biz. After the job, I ended up getting an apartment in the Crittendon Hotel off of Lincoln Park and Lake Shore

Drive. It had a Murphy bed, small kitchen, and living room on the fifth floor. It was within walking distance from the Walton Street Playboy Club. When I went to the club I walked down Rush Street past the Saint Valentine Day massacre garage. (That was spooky!) I also signed up with some modeling agencies in the Chicago area. That gave me other jobs outside of Playboy, and that was okay with them. I was in a world that was unfamiliar to me and I really didn't know where to start. But each morning when I woke up I couldn't wait to get out into this new world that had something exciting everyday! My old faithful, basketball pushed me to the Lawson YMCA. I started shooting baskets and meeting other ballplayers. We began organizing a team. It was just like New York. You go to a local bar, tell them that the whole team will come into the bar after each game if the owner would sponsor the team. The owner said, "yes." The bar, was just down the street from the YMCA off Chicago Avenue. It was called the Clover Leaf. Some of the ballplayers who I met worked for the Chicago Stock Exchange. Others were just jocks. We started winning. What might have helped was having the models and Bunnies coming to the games as we progressed through the season, to cheer us on. What a life! Plus we ended up winning the league.

Basketball was the love of my life, and after the Knicks dropped me and the season was over, I found out that Red Holtzman was to be the next new coach of the New York Knicks. The urge to try again emerged, knowing that Red Holtzman liked me. However, at that time, I didn't know that I was going to be in the world of Playboy. That probably is the only thing that would keep me from trying again. How can a single man ever turn that away? So much for a basketball career…

My exposure in Playboy magazine was leading me to a lot of outside jobs. One with Vic Skrebniski Studios and a model named Wilhemina. She later started one of the largest modeling agencies in New York City. Vic Skrebniski was one of the top photographers in the country. When you worked for him it was an honor. He had an assistant by the name of Wood Keuysumi. After one of the shootings, Woody asked me if I would be interested in doing some test shots with him? He was starting a portfolio to go out on his own. I said I would, and I could always use the new pictures anyway. After that we became good friends. We would go on fishing trips, play pool, get drunk and argue about Pearl Harbor.

Finally he got his own studio on the top floor of a beauty salon, a great location; where he did Barbara Streisand's first album cover. I was there during the shooting and thought to myself, this girl will never make it. What do I know? Woody's studio became a regular meeting place for partying, which kept growing in size because of the location, plus, the lure of a photo studio. When we added strip poker to our events, things really got hot. We ended up calling it The Love Shack. There were plenty of other parties in Chicago that I went to that had all kinds of drugs. All these young kids were puffing away on all kinds of instruments of pleasure. I still don't know why they do it. They don't have any problems and haven't even started living yet. I guess it's peer pressure, but many of them get hooked and their lives become questionable.

Playboy In Paris

I was going on a job for Playboy to Paris, Illinois, from Chicago, with three girls and one other male model. I was sitting in the back of the van and next to me was a model who just finished doing the cover of Playboy. We talked for a while, and the further we got away from the city, the more she came on to me. We were in full necking form when the other models started to interrupt us. They saw that it was getting sloppy. We arrived at the motel. I thought this was going to be a sure thing. The other models thought that we should play a joke on Don Braunstein, the photographer. I think the purpose was just to break us up. The cover girl and I would hide, and the others would go and tell Braunstein that we were intimate and maybe had run off. We hid behind the shower curtain in my room. Braunstein came in and couldn't find us. He was getting nervous. It got to the point that we had to reveal ourselves before he called Hef. He didn't appreciate it, but boys and girls will be (boys). The next day we left for the location, which was a county fair, outside Paris, Illinois. There were tents all over the place. We went into one with five models and two photographers and their assistants. We saw the ugliest girls on a bar, squatting down and picking up quarters with their wombs. The girl's left immediately, we stayed a little longer. The photographers had a ball. The next day's location was on a large raft on a lake where the girls were wearing skimpy bikinis. It was very difficult to concentrate on the job, but the shooting went well. Now it's time to go back to Chicago. We all got back in the van. I sat next to the cover girl, who I didn't get to go to bed with. We got into necking again, but as we approached Chicago, she started pushing me away. When we arrived it was like she didn't even know me. I guess some girls, when they get away from home, become someone else. That job ended up on the cutting room floor, like a lot of them did; but we still got paid. Another shooting was at Hefner's mansion Pool, three beautiful models and me. The girl spent almost all day having their hair and makeup done, but in my mind, that stuff didn't register. I pushed one of the girls into the pool before the shooting. If you've ever seen a beautiful girl go crazy, you had to see this one! The photographer didn't get mad. He told me to please let him know before I did it again. It didn't work. The girls were too fast. After the shooting, I did let them throw me into the pool. (What fun!).

I did a lot of illustration work back in New York. Most of it was for the covers of paperback books. At one time, if you looked at a rack of books, my image was on a quarter of them. I also got the opportunity to do the billboard for the movie Cleopatra. I wore the tunic and the sword. Richard Burton's head was then put on my body. They did the same with the female model, and Liz Taylor. It was on the cover of Esquire magazine. I received a call from my mother in New York and she told me I was famous. It seems the model and aspiring actress, jumped on something Liz Taylor said about the

Billboard shooting and found herself on the Johnny Carson show. They showed the original picture of the two of us posing for the billboard picture. It was in all the New York papers. The next day it came out in the Chicago papers, always one day behind. It said Richard Bennett and Lois Bennett, no relation, posing for the largest billboard ever, on Time

Square etc. etc. The publicity was great for me.

Young girls were coming into Chicago trying to be a model or a Bunny. There were so many available that I didn't know who to take advantage of first. I felt I had power over most girls. Of course, it was because I was with Playboy, and most girls wanted to be involved some way or another. If I didn't know better, I'd thought that I had the "Love Potion Number Nine".

Occasionally, I would go up to Patricia Stevens modeling agency, to see if any checks had come in for me. This one time there was a group of prospective models there, just getting ready to leave. So I took the opportunity to walk down the stairs with them, starting a conversation with one of the girls, teasing her on how young she looked. She quickly replied "oh yeah" as if she's been around the world a few times. So I jumped on that opening, suggesting we go up to my apartment, she replied, "show me the way". I grabbed her hand and couldn't get into bed fast enough, everything went well until she told me that she was pregnant. The shock of that statement led me to believe that I was getting involved into something that I shouldn't. She then explained the story that she left Ohio when she found out that she was pregnant. Not even telling her boyfriend, obviously she was confused and she just wanted to get away from the problems at hand. It seemed that she needed someone to talk to, she talked about everything. It was confusing to me, but I listened. Now I had to come up with something to help her. I gave it a try by telling her that you just have to believe that it's going to work. At least give it a try. Things will pan out, and you'll look back on it after a year or so as a learning experience. I guess it worked, because she decided to go back home and see. (Somehow I felt like I did something good for a change.)

Dating A Playboy Centerfold

One of the high points of my life was at a basketball game in Chicago. It was a game between the New York Knicks and the Detroit Pistons; a doubleheader. The second game was Chicago and another team. Dick Maguire, Coach of Detroit, an ex-New York Knick Captain and in the Hall of Fame, was a good friend of mine. He left tickets at the door for my basketball friends and me. Before the game started, I walked down to the floor at half court. Dick came over to me, and while I was talking to him, the Knicks players, as they were warming up, came over to me and shook my hand. They must have seen my pictures in Playboy. I thought to myself, who is the star now? (That's right). That's what I was really thinking. I invited all of the Detroit players to the Playboy club that night. Danny Doyle, one of the Detroit players, used to play with me on the local Killian's team back in Queens, New York. I was also thinking that it would give me a good opportunity to take a Playboy centerfold with me to the club by the name of Sherolee Conners, Playmate of July 1961. In fact, I fell in love with her picture before I even met her. I would go to sleep with her picture next to my pillow. Previously in my life I tried to be invisible, but as I progressed through life, I changed, especially when I got involved with Playboy and gained a lot more confidence. I asked Sherolee if she wanted to go with me? I couldn't believe that she was even talking to me. She said yes. She had to get an okay from Playboy's office. They were very strict about dating customers and fraternizing, but they did say yes, thank you.

I was hoping that taking her to the Playboy club to meet the Detroit Pistons would perhaps impress her. The Detroit team was mesmerized when they met her and I was proud as a peacock. The guys know what I mean.

The next day I was asked to go up to the Playboy offices, where I was presented with my Playboy key. The girls came up with the only number that would represent some kind of sex symbol. It was C13069, "C" stands for celebrity. Wow! I felt like I had finally made it. One thing about the girls at the

Playboy's office is that they always had fun. The last time I was there, as I was leaving, I got onto the elevator, and one of the girls got in behind me.

We were just going down from the second floor to the first. Low and behold, the elevator stopped between floors. It reminded me of one of the cartoons in Playboy, where this couple was stuck for quite a while and decided to have sex, so I said, "are we supposed to make love now?" She laughed, and said, "I don't think we have time." The elevator started to move, when the door opened all the girls were there. I don't know what they expected to see, but we all had a good laugh. The people who worked for Playboy knew that they were working for a magazine that doubled the circulation of any other magazine in the world and they were proud of it. These were the golden years of Playboy, and I was part of it.

When I write about myself, I'm not trying to build myself up, I'm trying to tell my story, thoughts and feelings; what I remember. This includes things that are important to me and things that I would do over if I had the chance.

Dinner with a Playmate

I took Sherolee to the VIP room for dinner at the Playboy club in Chicago. The dinner took about three hours. During that time, I got to know my date. I wasn't much of a talker, but I found some things to talk about, mostly my past, or something interesting that I was involved in at that time. She liked to talk, and told me the story about how Playboy wanted her for their centerfold. It went like this - There was a photographer in New York who was recruiting for Playboy and he told her that she was the perfect type they were looking for and the money they offered was very good also. After thinking about it for a couple of weeks, she agreed to do it. One of the first things that she wanted done was changing her name from Karolee Bowman to Sherolee Connors, taking the last name from her grandmother. She also told me about the time Hef took her out to a show, like he did with all the new playmates.

This time, he took her to the Copacabana Nightclub in New York, where Andy Williams was the act that night. After the show, Andy Williams took Hef and Sherolee to his apartment to show off his art collection. It was a great night for her and Hef was a perfect gentleman. Great story. Then Sherolee took a pause in our conversation to leave the table to powder her nose. While she was gone, a girl from one of the other tables came over to me and asked me for my autograph. She had seen my pictures in Playboy, and in ads. She sat down at the table waiting for me to sign her paper. I was thinking I'd better hurry up. I didn't want Sherolee to see this girl at the table. She might get jealous or angry. I just didn't want anything to disturb this date. I always felt like a jerk signing my name. What do they do with these things anyway? Like the kids at the New York Knicks training camp, they didn't even know who I was but still asked anyway. Sherolee came back to the table. I think the girl was aware of my situation and left. When I met a girl who I really liked, I tried to impress her with some way to remember our meeting. I used music. At that time, a "Summer Place" was the hot number, so I took that as our theme song. She liked it. It was a very successful night. After that we dated and would go to our favorite coffee shop, which had a jukebox. I would play a "Summer Place" every time we went in. One time we had an argument and went into the coffee shop, not saying anything until, to our surprise; the song came on. The manager had played it. It settled things right down. I suggest this as a part of a relationship to all young lovers. When I dated Sherolee I didn't press her for sex, because I didn't want her to think that's all I was after. Let it come naturally. (It worked!)

Close Call
After one of our basketball workouts, the whole team

went to a bar that had dancing. The twist was the big thing then and I loved it. The dance teacher asked me if I would do a routine with her on the stage. Her name was Evelyn. All of the guys pushed me up onto the stage. I figured it was just innocent fun, so I did the twist with her. Of course there was a bunny in the audience who couldn't wait to tell Sherolee that I was with another woman. When I returned home that night, Sherolee called and asked if I knew a girl named Evelyn? She caught me off guard, I said no. She said that's all I wanted to know and hung up. That bunny was fired. That was close.

A Fishing Trip With A Playmate

I loved fishing and would go up to Wisconsin to fish fresh water. One time I was just about to leave when Sherolee asked if she could go with me? I couldn't turn that down, so I said "yes, sure!" Off we went. The white fish were running in mid Wisconsin rivers as we arrived at our destination. There were people on both sides, pulling in the fish left and right. I worked my way to an open spot and began to fish. I started catching fish immediately. Sherolee thought it looked like fun. She asked me if she could try? I said o.k. and handed her the rod. Just about that time, a game warden came up to Sherolee and asked her for her license. She looked at me. I told the warden that I had a license and that she was just keeping me company. The warden stated that she was holding a fishing rod. He insisted that we go to the courthouse with him. I couldn't believe it! Sherolee started angrily saying, "I'll call Hef!" I told her to keep quiet. If they knew about Hef, they would make a bigger thing of this. She agreed. We went to what looked like a little private house. We walked in to see a man sitting behind a large desk, looking like a judge.   It appeared that they had set up a temporary courthouse for the opening of the fishing season. They probably made a good buck for the town. He asked how much we had. I told him. He took all of my cash, except for $5.00. I had a quarter of a tank of gas; Sherolee said again that we should call Hef. I said "no!" If you know how men are, I can make it without help. In those days we had no credit cards or cell phones, how did we survive? Off we went with the gas tank hanging on empty. It seemed like it took forever, looking at the gas gauge and growing hungrier by the minute. Finally, Sherolee said, "I can't take it. I'm hungry. Let's stop and get something." We gambled and did, by eating a couple of hamburgers and blowing the $5.00. The gamble worked and somehow we made it without calling Hef for help. It was an incredible trip with her, no matter what we did. Just being with her made me feel good, like a high, I couldn't wait to see her again. (I think I'm falling in love!)

Chapter 9: Playboy Mansion

Hef's parties on Friday night were the big thing. All the celebrities who were in town were there. I had a thrill to see and meet them all. They were people who you see on a screen in a movie, but didn't think they existed in real life. It was a funny feeling. Finally Hef would come in wearing his red smoking jacket and holding his pipe. He walked around saying hello to everyone and then disappeared. After awhile I was walking down the hall looking for the men's room. When I passed by Hef's bedroom, the door was open. There he was. I could see what he really was in love with. It was the Playboy magazine. The papers were strewn all over the bed. He would work all night. It seems that he could think more clearly, without the business of the day all over him. He did look up and pointed me towards the men's room. When the party began to fade, we would go to other parties that loved to have the overflow from Hef's. A lot of pros would sing, comedians would do their thing and we would go on until 10 a.m. or 12 noon. We would then stop for breakfast in the local diners. They would put gin or vodka in coffee cups for that last nightcap. (We were night people.)My son came to Chicago to visit with me for a week. He was about nine years old. I took him to the zoos and ball games, but the highlight was taking him to the Playboy Mansion to swim in Hef's pool, which was okay with Hef. The pool had two levels. If you swam to the bottom you could look into the bar through a large glass window and if you wanted to get into the bar from the pool level you could slide down a fireman's pole. There were all kinds of game machines. My son had a blast! That's something he can talk about for years; his day at the Playboy Mansion. Unfortunately, for many reasons my son and I lost whatever relationship we once had. Hef's Mansion Pool was the scene of another job with a girl photo director, overlooking the job. I was lying down with a beautiful girl by the name of Arlene Drake in a bikini, who was an aspiring actress. It was a

close shot. The female director kept telling me to jump into the pool and cool off. I don't know how these guys do this type of scene without getting excited. Another job at the beach found me having to throw a beach ball to a playmate and making her top come off. Another shot at the Playboy Mansion was called "Playboys Party Games". There was one scene where Hef's new

Above: Game of catch has delightful catch to it as player outleaps bikini.

girlfriend was in the shot. I was blindfolded and had to find a

69

person and reveal their identity. The photographer told me where to go and what to grab, so I did. He got the shot, and I got slapped. Afterwards, she got even with me and I didn't even know it! With my eyes closed, I thought she was running her finger all over my face, instead it was lipstick.

The Living Room was a nightclub that came to Chicago from New York. Owner, Danny Siegel, had two clubs there called the Living Room and the Phone Booth. Danny and I became good friends in Chicago. I would get him models for luncheons and fashion shows; Sherolee would get him some discontented Bunnies. One night I dropped by the club. They had a bar that you could look through a soundproof glass window to see the show without disturbing anyone. Danny spotted me at the bar and came out and said to me, "I have someone I want you to meet." He brought out Denise Darcel, the French actress. She had just finished a picture with Gary Cooper and Burt Lancaster. She was big at that time. He introduced me to her. She gave me a kiss on the cheek. I searched for something to say like, "you were so great in your last picture." It always comes out dumb.

Another time, Sherolee and I went to see a show at the same club. When we sat down, a bottle of champagne was brought to our table from Danny. After the show was over, we were invited to stay in a private room with Tony Bennett, Al Hirt, his singer and a gentleman by the name of Frank. He asked me how were things in New York? It was like he wasn't allowed there. Curious, I sat next to Tony. I told him that I knew his brother's place in Queens, New York. He had a hair salon. Tony responded, "yeah", and that was it. I guess he didn't like being there, so I turned my back and had fun listening to Al Hirt tell jokes. (Great night!)

Keys To The City

When Sherolee became a centerfold, she also had to do promotional work for Playboy Magazine, like go to St. Louis, where the mayor and Ed Carr, of the St. Louis Hawks N.B.A. basketball team; gave her the key to the city. Her job was to present a birthday gift to Bob Petet, the top scorer for the Hawks team. At the presentation, after the gift was given, all the fans cheered for her to kiss him, so she did. Another key to the city was given to her in Beaumont, Texas, where she signed autographs at the Naval School. When she came back to Chicago, she stayed at the Playboy Mansion. She was assigned to the Blue Room and she turned in early. Later that night she heard a noise. Someone was coming into her room; from the light of the open door she could see it was Hef. She didn't know what to do. So she turned over and stretched. Hef quickly left the room and then all the lights on the phone lit up. Obviously, he was in the wrong room. (That was close!)

Sherolee received mail from all over the world. She received an invitation to Steve Allen's Tonight Show, which she accepted. She then got love letters, proposals of marriage, dirty letters and movie calls. One of the letters was for a movie being shot in Europe with a high budget, called Goldfinger. That sounded very suspicious, so she threw it away with the rest of the junk mail. (Little did we know!)

Playboy Offices

On another occasion at the Playboy offices in the main building, waiting for a photographer, I was told that he would be at least a half hour late. So to kill some time, the girls let me into a room that had file cabinets all around; a white on white room. This is where all the pictures were stored of those who wanted to become Playmates. They told me to entertain myself, so I started looking. There were old girls, young girls, ugly and beautiful ones, thousands from all over the world. Very few people ever get to see this. I started to realize that I had the job that every man would give his right arm for. Here are some of my *full-page* pictures that I did for Playboy:

THE LONG AND THE SHORT OF IT
quick-change artistry: a double-entendre in summerwear

(That's me getting tackled)

THE ONE-BUTTON SUIT

Below: Gang engages in a bit of upbeat isometrics entitled "Twist Until You Drop." Portable hi-fi supplies the sound while sole survivors of the twistathon keep in the swing of things.

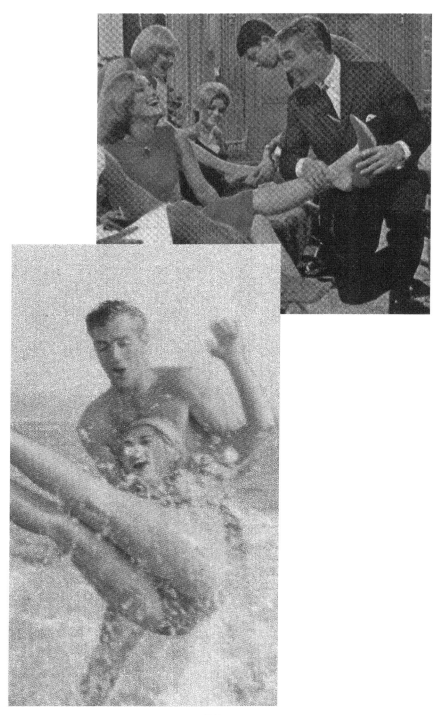

attire By ROBERT L. GREEN "For my part," wrote Robert Louis Stevenson, "I travel not to go anywhere, but to go. I travel for travel's sake. The great affair is to move." Whatever their wont, idol-worshiping Americans in growing numbers seem to feel the same stirrings of wanderlust for the open road as the place to spend their holidays—sampling the pleasures of peregrination from beach to bosque, from mountain to metropolis. Thanks to accelerating advancements in automobile design and engineering, to the mushrooming of luxury motels from coast to coast, and to the proliferation of high-speed turnpikes which have brought the scenic side routes of everything but hitherto inaccessible spots within easy reach, the road to summertime sojourns by car has never been so high, wide and handsome. Neither has the wardrobe of the travel-wise male materialize—as evidenced by the sartorial tour *(concluded on page 106)*

For radio & scenic aerial shot of man was nape-in breezy wind breaker for top-down turnpike travel.

With the mercury pushing 80°, my funny valentine

"warms" himself by a cold motel fireplace.

Decked out for dinner at roadside inn, he loses

his head completely over my snappy camerawork.

True shot of me proves he's a gifted photog. Mine prove she has the gift of garb.

For further information on Illustrated men's attire, see info on page 106

I flips tom-tit in the lonely T-Bird for takeoff.

He flips mine in cool white cardigan and blank slacks.

Our swinging vacation begun—and so for my grope as a shutterbug

During dealer imagery, but is it art? My mate suited entire takes five bird ... & decided for the nines.

GEARED FOR TOURING
SOME CANDID PORTRAITS OF A FREEWHEELING AND FASHIONABLE MOTOR TRIP

only fashion white, denim breaker and groovy loafers

82

TV Commercials

Another photo shoot was for a TV commercial with a beautiful model. It was for a hair product. The shooting was going along nicely until the art director decided that we should try a kissing scene. The model made it clear that she only kissed her husband. The art director suggested we take a break and asked me to see if I could try to change her mind. I opened up by telling her that kissing a model is nothing, it's like kissing your mother, without any sexual thoughts. (Sure!) Then I asked her just to try one little kiss. I leaned over and gave her a quick one. I didn't want to scare her. Saying to her; "that's all we have to do". She finally agreed. We started shooting again. After the fifth take, the art director said, "it was getting too sloppy." How about that?

Because of my background of basketball, Wilson sporting goods asked me to do two TV commercials. One was for golf, which I didn't play, but the girl who I was supposed to be with in the commercial knew how, so she said; but she really didn't. They asked me to try. I hit the ball, but couldn't get it in the air. They said that was okay and the finished product didn't look bad at all. The second was a tennis commercial. All I had to do was run and chase the ball, which I could do.

It opened the door to other commercials. I still wouldn't do anything with speaking lines, because I still had a complex about reading in front of people. Too bad. That slowed up my career.

Falling In Love

Thinking back, I had one girl after another, not really caring about anyone until I fell in love. Love is that I want to be with her **all** the time. That feeling in the pit of your stomach that you want to touch and kiss and hug her, afraid of all of the men getting too close for comfort. All these feelings are love, but the hard part is keeping it.

Marriage # 2 (1961)

Getting ready to ask for Sherolee's hand in marriage, I tried to figure a way that if she said no, I wouldn't feel like a jerk. It reminds me of when I was back in school. I wouldn't ask a girl to dance or talk to a girl because she might say no and that would be devastating. I thought, what am I, a baby? Just ask, so I said, "how would you like to get married?" She laughed and said, "yes!" That didn't hurt. Sherolee and I ran off and got married quietly. Most of the people we knew didn't even know for a long time that we were married. We weren't sure how Playboy would react also.

Chapter 10: Cover Of Playboy Magazine

ENTERTAINMENT FOR MEN

DECEMBER ONE DOLLAR

PLAYBOY

SPECIAL CHRISTMAS GIFT ISSUE WITH ANNIVERSARY ISSUE

CHRISTMAS CARTOONS
HUMOR & SATIRE BY
JULES FEIFFER
SHEL SILVERSTEIN
ELDON DEDINI
ALBERTO VARGAS
GAHAN WILSON
E. SIMMS CAMPBELL
ERICH SOKOL
JOHN DEMPSEY
PHIL INTERLANDI
PLUS A SIX-PAGE
PLAYBOY PICTORIAL
ON ARLENE DAHL &
A PHOTO UNCOVERAGE
OF "PLAYBOY'S OTHER
GIRLFRIENDS,"—
SOPHIA LOREN
KIM NOVAK
BRIGITTE BARDOT
ANITA EKBERG

CHRISTMAS FEATURES
FACT & FICTION BY
JAMES THURBER
RAY BRADBURY
LUDWIG BEMELMANS
RUDY VALLEE
NELSON ALGREN
RICK RUBIN
GARSON KANIN
ART BUCHWALD
SHEPHERD MEAD
ERNIE KOVACS
HUGH M. HEFNER
PLUS "PLAYBOY'S
HOLIDAY PUNCH,"
& "THE CHRISTMAS
DINNER FLAMBÉ,"
BY THOMAS MARIO WITH
NINE COLOR PAGES
OF CHRISTMAS GIFT
SUGGESTIONS FOR MEN

We had no idea how Marilyn Monroe's untimely death would impact the lives of Sherolee and myself. Marilyn had been contracted to do the Christmas cover of Playboy Magazine, December 1962. It was to be a different type of cover. Playboy had advanced ideas in photography. Given that it was the 1960's; we were more than excited when Sherolee was asked to take Marilyn's place on the cover. I was at the shooting. They had two white paper drops at each end of the studio with a hole for the camera lens. I was behind one end with Don Braunstein and another photographer was at the other end of the studio. There would be a count to three, and both would shoot as Sherolee changed her pose each time they shot. Her body was judiciously draped in a white ermine stole with Christmas presents at her feet. The final result was a transparent cover with Sherolee face front. When the cover was turned, it was her backside. In those years, much was left to the imagination of the beholder.

Chicago To New York For My Sister's Wedding

Remember, my sister Barbara was the one who was going to marry me. Sherolee and I drove to New York. Before that, I had lost my wallet on the beach and didn't have time to get a new drivers license. We attended the wedding, and it was great. On the way back on the Pennsylvania Turnpike, I stopped for gas. Sherolee wasn't feeling well and was lying down in the back seat. I asked her if she wanted to go to the ladies' room. She declined. I ran to the men's room. When I returned, there was a line of cars behind mine. I quickly paid for the gas and jumped into the car and drove off. About 50 miles down the turnpike I was speeding along, making good time until I heard the sound of a siren. A cop pulled me over in a red, unmarked car. He asked for my license and registration (shit). I told him I had lost my wallet, but I had a YMCA card.

He laughed and told me to step out of the car. He asked where I was going and I told him, Chicago; with my wife. He asked where she was. I told him she was not feeling well and was in the backseat lying down. As I looked into the backseat, I almost had cardiac arrest, as she wasn't there! The cop grabbed me by the arm and said, "come with me." I pulled away and got very angry. He saw that I was very upset and finally told me that my wife had called the police and told us that I had left her at the gas station. The cop admitted to me that he wouldn't have pulled me over if she hadn't called, so he helped me to make a U-turn on the Pennsylvania Turnpike and head back to the gas station. When I finally got back and picked her up, she sat next to me and didn't let go of my arm. The story went like this. I left a Playboy centerfold on the Pennsylvania Turnpike. How about that?

My Brother's Honeymoon

My brother, Ed, was going on his honeymoon by boat from the New York Harbor to the islands. Everyone was partying. There was lots of drinking and dancing on board. I was with Sherolee. When it was time for all the guests to leave the boat, the bell was rung, but I didn't want to get off. I was well inebriated. I wanted to go with Ed and his wife, Jean, on their honeymoon. They finally convinced me to get off. We began throwing streamers from the dock onto the boat as our farewell gesture. It was then that a group of teenage girls who were on the boat, started asking me questions, like was I a piano player on another ship, or a singer? I guess they must have thought I was someone because of Sherolee by my side. They were closing in on me, like a group of cattle, when Sherolee stepped in between us. Can you imagine that? Having a Playboy centerfold protect you from a group of teenage girls, in the condition I was in? I still had the mental capacity to take a flower from my lapel and throw it. All the girls started running for it. That gave Sherolee and me a chance to run down the stairs and out to the parking lot. This was another of life's strong moments. I don't envy the big stars.

New York Playboy Club

Sherolee opened the New York Playboy Club on 59th Street and Fifth Avenue in 1962.

(Bunny Mother and me)

Bunny Mother Sherolee

She hired all the Bunnies and was known as the Bunny Mother. The picture on right shows her serving me. She trained them and even gave them demerits for wearing their ears wrong or their tails crooked. Everything had to be just right. She also hired Gloria Steinem, who went undercover as a Bunny to do the inside story of the New York Playboy Club. That started what was to be a career of a well-known author.

I would occasionally go to the New York Club from Chicago. One time while I was there in Sherolee's, office, which was in the Bunny locker room, I hit it right on the head. It was payday. I was sitting next to Sherolee at her desk when she announced that all the checks were ready. The girls all rushed into the office, some wearing no tops, some no bottoms, giving me dirty looks. That's when Sherolee made it clear that it was the last time I would be allowed into the office.

89

(It wasn't my fault.) I went back to Chicago, where things began getting distant between us, because of the geographies, the temptations, and the whole lifestyle.

Wanted In Europe

I did a lot of catalog work, most of which was sent to Europe. A firm in Europe liked my look and wanted me for their catalog. They offered me a one-year contract to do their catalog and wear their clothes to different parties in various countries in Europe, with a beautiful escort. I told them my wife was a centerfold, and a cover girl for Playboy. They said, "great! The gentleman who had the job before me had worked ten years on a one-year at a time contract. The offer was a hundred grand and expenses. This was the job every model was looking for in those days. I called Sherolee in New York and told her all about the job offer. Her response was, "is that all you think of me, as something to show off?" I slammed the phone down and went to the Playboy Club and tried to get drunk. One interesting aside was that I got to meet Charleston Heston. That evening the manager came up to me at the bar and asked me how it felt to be sitting next to Moses. I said, "Moses who?" I turned and looked into the face of Charleston Heston. He said, "it's me." It seems he came into the club and the Bunny at the front door wouldn't let him in because he didn't have a key. Some club members came by the door and invited him in as their guest. They all sat next to me at the bar and questioned him about the chariot race in the Ben Hur movie. After I had enough of that, I headed home. When I arrived, the manager told me that my wife was coming in at O'Hare Airport. Somehow I made it out there on time.

My heart was pounding at the thought of seeing her. Finally she came through the passenger exit, and I rushed to her with tears in my eyes, hugging like two lovers meeting after a long period of separation. Yes, absence does make the heart grow fonder. What a wonderful feeling, and "Summer Place" was being played on the speaker system. This was what we needed, to get out of the business and start a fresh new life together. I pretty much had it with this kind of life anyway, and wanted to get back to reality. We planned to buy a house in New Jersey and start a family. This was a big turn in the road. I'd given up the European job, because I felt I'd get into trouble anyway. We were going to make this work or try damn hard at it. Thinking about it, I was looking forward to working on home projects, doing the things that I enjoyed with my hands again. Playboy still called us; it was hard to turn them down. Our love began there, and we thank them for bringing us together. *"Thank You, Playboy!"*

Chapter 11: Move For Love

We moved to a little town in New Jersey, by the name of Pequannock, not far from my mother and father's house. This brought us closer by doing things together with them, like playing cards. Golfing with my father made us buddies. Karolee (which is Sherolee's real name) and I played softball with the local teams. We went to church on Sundays, just like most people in town.

Playboy kept calling. They wanted me for a one-week shooting in L.A. It still was hard to turn down, but we did. I took a job with W. T. Grants in Clark, New Jersey, managing their six bay auto department off of the Garden State Parkway. I was also asked to become a Commissioner with the Pequannock's Parks and Recreation Department. I was honored, the first thing I did was starting a night basketball league to keep the boys off the streets; thinking of my past. I also wondered what happened to the kids who didn't make the high school basketball team. I guess it must be rather depressing when you really want something, but there's no place for you, so we started a league using these boys. We called it the Triboro League with teams from all around the North Jersey area. I took the job as coach. The boys who I had were 15 and 16 years of age who loved the game. I had to convince them that they were good enough to play with anyone. I worked with them one on one, playing with them, showing how to play defense and a little dirty play, like holding the other player when boxing out. The first game we played, everything was going well, until a timeout was called. The referee came to our huddle and told one of the boys that the next time he saw him holding he would call a foul. The boy looked at me. I told him to keep doing it. He didn't call a foul did he? Another time, one of my boys was getting pushed around. He was our high scorer. It was like the other team was trying to goad him into a fight. I told him not to do anything until the game was over, so sure enough, he decked the kid after the game. The head of the league called me and told me that I would have to let the boy go for fighting. I responded that if he had to go then so would I. So he said I'll get back to you. When he did, he told me that the boy would be given one more chance. That was great motivation for the team, knowing that I would stand behind them 100%. Our season ended by winning the league. I tried to get a game against the high school team, but they wouldn't play us. It would have been great for the boys, especially if they had won. What happened to the boys who didn't make the high school team? They won.

Grudge Game

Don Ryan called me and said that the town of Rutherford, New Jersey, where the Giants Stadium is located is having a grudge game against the Rutherford police department. They were undefeated in basketball. The town wanted Don Ryan from Atlanta Christian, Tom Fitzmaurice from St. Bonaventure and me from Bryant high school to be ringers for the town's team. They said they would pay us and I said ok. A week before the game I was in the backyard in the wintertime. I flipped a piece of wood that was on the ground with my foot. All of a sudden, I had a sharp pain in my lower back and fell to the ground. I couldn't move, I thought I was paralyzed. I tried to holler for someone, but the pain was excruciating. I was starting to get cold and was thinking this is serious. Finally, Lisa came out. Thank God, she called her mother and pulled me into the bar, which had a soft black shag rug and access to a bathroom. We called the doctor, he said, I pinched a nerve and to put compresses on it. I still couldn't move and all I could think about was the commitment that I made to the town of Rutherford. My father heard what happened and came over to the house. I was still on the floor in the bar. I tried crawling to the bathroom and caressing the toilet bowl trying to pull myself up, but ended up in a laughing fit. It's hard to explain, my father had this problem at one time himself and always felt that an enema would cure anything, who's the doctor here? He ended up giving me ten enemas. That's 10 bags of water up my ass. It seemed like it would never end (funny) then he said, one more bag and I said, "shit" (perfect word).

The next day came. I'm on my feet, wobbly, but improving. Before you knew it, it was time for the Rutherford basketball game. My father gave me one more adjustment, putting us back to back. Then he lifted me by bending over and something cracked. I felt better after that. My back was stiff, but walk able. On to the game… We all met at the coach's house in Rutherford, and drove to where the game was to be played. They had made sure the high school was blacked out and as we approached the gymnasium, the noise kept getting louder and louder. When we opened the door to the gym, the whole town was there, cheering us as we came in. It seemed the police didn't want this to be a sanctioned game. That's why all the lights were out and people parked in surrounding areas. As I was warming up, my back seemed to loosen up. The first half was okay. We were leading, and the town people were going crazy. The second half, I felt great, like I never had any problems at all. Near the end of the game, a guy I was guarding was a leaper. He drove towards me, I crouched over spreading my arms and he attempted to jump over me. I raised my arm to protect myself. His foot hit my hand, flipping him over hard and wouldn't you know it? He broke his arm! Now I'm in for it. They called for an ambulance, with no siren. We finished the game and won.

Afterward, we all went to a restaurant. I was sitting at the table with the other players. When the cop with the broken arm came in with a cast on, I thought to myself, (oh boy). He came over to the table and said, "nice game." How about that? My back is fine. Thanks dad!

Our Children

Karolee and I had two girls, Lisa and Jessica. Our home in Pequannock, was on three quarters of an acre; a tri-level. We built decks and a great room with a bar where we hung all our Playboy pictures, modeling pictures, Karolee's keys to the cities and my trophies. Of course, things just don't go smoothly. Karolee's grandmother was very ill, her mother wanted to put her into a home, but Karolee could not agree to that, instead she offered to take her into our home. I agreed. She walked into the house and was helped up the stairs. She never came down. I have never seen the love and devotion between two people as Karolee and her grandmother. Her grandmother needed shots and had to have her system cleared out regularly. Karolee would do that, until she finally passed away. We knew that we had lost a wonderful woman. That's something I'll always remember.

Story of the chicken

One Easter, Lisa and Jessica received a baby chicken, which we put up in a pen in the rear of our property. The girls loved it and fed it the best grain you could buy. The chicken grew to be a large white beauty. The only thing was when it started to lay eggs, they were so large that while the egg passed through the chicken's system it's innards came out with it. When the girls saw this, they screamed for me. I could think of nothing to do but to push the innards back into the chicken. That led the girls and me to the office of a veterinarian, where I sat with the chicken in my lap with all the other patrons in the room looking at me. I did this for the girls and they were watching me closely. I stood strong and waited my turn. The doctor said they would have to operate but afterward we had to lock up the chicken for days and hope that she didn't lay another egg. It worked! We changed the diet and all was better again. I was the girl's hero!

Horses

The girls loved horseback riding. One day the whole family decided to go riding. I really didn't care for it, but it was a family thing. Jessica was about four years old, so she sat on the horse with me. I held her with my left arm, and the reigns with my right hand. We were trotting along, following Karolee and Lisa, when all of a sudden there was an open field ahead of us. All the horses started running fast without command. I couldn't believe it. I thought the horse was going to step in a hole and we would go head over heels, while Jessica was hollering faster, daddy, faster. That little pipsqueak! Finally we reached some woods where they slowed to a walk. I swore I'd never do that again. The girls loved horses, but then, what young girl doesn't? As they grew up, they both worked part-time at

the riding Academy. Jessica invested all her money to purchase a horse and rent a stall at a stable close by, so her mother or sister could drive her there. One day she got me to take her to the farm. I was against her having something she really couldn't afford. When we arrived, Jessica stepped up onto the wooden fence. All the horses were out in the field. I didn't know which one was hers until she let out a call. One of the horses raised its tail and with a smooth prance came right up to her, pressing its head into Jessica's chest. It was one of the most beautiful things to see. Now I understood why she loved that horse.

W T Grants

The only exciting thing that happened there was one time someone robbed the cash register. It went like this; I was standing in the service area. The register was unattended, I happened to look back to the post that the register was behind. I saw someone's head peeking around it; I started toward the register, when a guy and a girl started running. The girl went one way and the guy went another. I decided to chase the guy. He ran to the front of the store. I hollered, "Stop him!" The manager tried to stop him, but was knocked down. That gave me just enough time to grab him in a headlock. While I was holding him, money was falling out of his pockets. All of a sudden, his head started shaking and he collapsed to the ground. It seemed he had a seizure and the girl got away. The police and ambulance came and took him away. Final results were they let him go because he didn't get out of the store with the money. What the hell are we trying to catch anyone for?

Chapter 12: Cheating

What makes us cheat? It could be boredom or non-communication, something like that, but most of the time it is someone who is outside the home who will listen to all your problems without any rebuttals of any kind. I believe once you cheat, it will happen again.

Here we go… this girl at work was going to get married, but was never with another man sexually. You guessed it, she asked me if I would go to bed with her so she would know what it was like with another man. I don't know if you could imagine this, but I said, "are you serious?" She said, "very." This was perfect at this time because of friction at home. She was Spanish and had a great body, no strings attached. I got a motel room, and we did it quick and easy as possible. Not giving her fiancé, any competition. It was bad. That's good! After that I had no remorse, just one thought, getting away with it. Not long after that, WT Grants went bankrupt, so I had to start looking for the next change. My neighbor told me that I could get a job with this shipping company that he knew about. He really didn't think that I could handle that job, but he didn't know me. It was working the midnight shift from 7 p.m. to 7 a.m. Overtime was mandatory. The job was unloading trucks on steel platforms in winter. It was a three-month job. I had the option after that, if I qualified, to join the union or not when that time came. I selected not to. It was one of the hardest jobs I ever had, but I did it. I was always proud of the fact that I could do any type of job and have no fear of anyone else's thoughts. But there came a time that I had to question that. It was when some of the guys I used to play basketball with were standing outside a bar. I was passing by in a car with some of my co-workers from the truck-loading job I was doing at the time. I thought that they were looking right at me as we went by. For some reason, I ducked down. I guess I was afraid that they might think I wasn't doing well, after seeing me in Playboy. I was probably embarrassed about what I was doing. (I guess I'm not so proud after all?)

Times Square

I became involved with a friend of mine to open a Rent-A-Car franchise on Times Square, one of the most filmed and visited streets in the world. Here I am right in the middle of it getting to know all the theater people like the June Taylor dancers, and all the crazy people who made it tick. The Rent-A-Car business was thriving, sold out every weekend. It was something that all the theater people and tourists could use, however the New York police were giving us a hard time. There are two police precincts crossing over Times Square. One we paid off every week and the other wouldn't accept payment. When all the cars came back on Monday morning, the police would stand there giving tickets to the cars that we couldn't get off the street fast enough. That made things tough.

Under Times Square

I had to go into work early one morning to do some paperwork. While I was looking out the front window at all the people walking by, busily going about their business, I saw a man coming up out of one of the metal covers on the sidewalk in front of the store and he walked off. A coworker and I decided to investigate and went down through the same opening in the street, with our flashlights shining everywhere. We found large steam pipes that made eerie sounds. It was scary, but we moved on with scrambling noises all around us. We came upon a room with unlit candles all over and food hanging in bags from the ceiling, I guess to keep the rats from getting it? A dirty makeshift bed and a box of things made it livable. This guy was living free under Times Square. We called the police. I don't know what happened to him, but we put a lock on the cover and wondered how many other people are living under the streets of Manhattan.

One evening after work, Bill, my coworker asked if I would go with him to a bar around the corner? I agreed, but the bar was a dingy place with a few people in it. We sat down and were immediately joined by a lady who somehow got into our conversation. All of a sudden I was going with her to a third-floor walk-up, and before you knew it we were in bed. It was great sex, and that was that. A week later, I decided to return to the scene of the crime. I rang the bell for another interlude, she answered. I introduced myself saying, "remember me from last week?" I was surprised, when in a loud voice she hollered over the intercom. "Go away!" and hung up. Boy that hurt! I walked away with my tail between my legs. That's New York for you.

One of the Rent-A-Car counter girls named Val was having a hard time finding which way she wanted to go in life, with girls or guys. Finally she decided against girls. The only problem was the girl she was going with didn't like the decision that she had made. The girlfriend was a little Spanish dyke who carried a switchblade. One night at work I could see that Val was very nervous and upset. So I asked her what was wrong. She replied she was going to meet the dyke at a diner on Times Square. I told her I would drop by after I closed up. What was I getting into? I walked up to the diner and could see inside through the glass window. The two of them were sitting at the counter. I took a deep breath and walked up to them and asked if everything was okay? I heard a click. It was that little shit and her knife; Val stood up between us and said everything's ok. I glared at that little shit and walked away slowly. I never knew if Val decided to stay with her or not. We just didn't talk about it anymore.

Someone came up with the idea about opening a Rent-A-Car service at LaGuardia Airport. So we gave it a try, I went out there to start the project, but to my surprise, I fell into a den of iniquity! During that month, I met all the airline stewardesses, most of whom room together sharing apartments. After we got familiar with each other, I was invited to some of their parties. I found it was nothing for one of the girls to grab you by the hand and take you into the bedroom during the party. It seems when these girls get away from home, anything goes, which I have experienced before. One of these girls, for some reason, would rather go to a motel, so we made arrangements to meet one Saturday and spent a full day in the motel. She was one of the loudest girls I've ever known. Finally it was over, heading home the guilt set in but that only lasted a short time before the urge arrives again. That's life…

One of our countermen worked at the Peppermint Lounge nightclub on the weekends. He told us that the Beatles were coming to the club to see the band that was imitating them. So we all went the night that they were there. One of the guitar players used a toilet seat as his instrument. They still sounded just like the Beatles. It was great. It was a night to remember, seeing the Beatles close up and in person.

Chapter 13: Another Road

After a year of running the Rent-a-Car business, the tickets from the second precinct caught up with us. We had to let the business go. What a great experience during that time. We had come to know most of our neighbors, like the Lincoln dealer across the street. I was closing the store up for good when one of the sales guys from the car dealer walked by and asked if I was closing up early? I told him it was for good. He asked, what I was going to do? I told him I had no idea. He replied that he had just had a gentleman buy a new Lincoln from him for cash, and he was looking for a driver. I responded that I didn't know a thing about chauffeuring. The salesman asked me to please do him a favor. He said the man with the Lincoln is at the 21 Club. He's tall, with gray hair and a patch over one eye. His name is Mr. Renaldo from Venezuela. Please just take the car over there and talk with him. I agreed to do it. I called home and explained what happened to Karolee. She told me to go for it. The salesman gave me a chauffeur's hat and off I went. I found a nice parking spot in front of Richard Bennett's clothing store (no relation), which was annexed to the 21 Club. I waited for Ronaldo to come out. He finally did. I introduced myself. He told me the next time I was to park in front of the 21. Oh boy! What a start.

I felt like a servant and didn't know if I was willing to continue, but he paid me cash and was very generous. He also liked the young debutantes. He would go to all the top clubs in Manhattan. He was married, but his wife was a staunch Catholic and would not divorce him. He had a reputation for being a worldwide playboy. One day Ronaldo said, "guess who I'm going riding with tomorrow?" Of course I had no idea. He proudly told me it was Jacqueline Kennedy. They were to meet at the Phipps estate on Long Island. The next day we arrived at the estate, which was magnificent. When Jacqueline arrived, she was driving a station wagon with her riding habit on, ready to go. Off they went.

Ronaldo had a hundred room villa in Venezuela, a house in the South of France, and an apartment on Park Avenue. Not too bad. Jacqueline has good taste, but nothing happened. I think his wife was the problem. I came to know most of his dates in the short six months that I worked for him. I must admit that I had a good time and learned a lot.

Senator Henry Cabot Lodge, Jr. (U.S. Representative to the United Nations, 1953-1960) also visited Ronaldo at his Park Avenue apartment. After their meeting, I drove him back to the Waldorf Astoria Hotel. As we were going down Park Avenue, we passed a chauffeur driven antique Rolls Royce whose passenger happened to be the famous American entrepreneur, Howard Johnson. Mr. Lodge said, "that is the height of hypocrisy," and laughed. I agreed, thinking that we almost expected to see a sign on the side of the Rolls stating, "Howard Johnson's."

The time came for Ronaldo to return home. He wanted my family and me to go with him to Venezuela. Enticing me with his large home and Rolls Royce. I started thinking about how it would be there, especially the kids, changing schools, languages, plus all the paperwork involved in the move. I told him, "no." Plus, Karolee said, "no." What a road that would have been...

The day came that I was to drive him to Kennedy Airport. One of his debutants was going with us. He told me, on the way back to the city, that I should ask her to have a drink with me. It seems as though she couldn't ask me herself. That would be too embarrassing, if I was to decline. I chickened out. When we stopped at her apartment, I didn't say anything. She threw a magazine up to the front of the car and said, "give this to your wife," and got out in a huff. I guess I did the right thing.

Now I had to look for new employment, but during this time at the Park Avenue apartments, I came to know all the people in the apartment complex. There were two families who wanted me to work for them. I decided to work for the Hill's. They had two children, Joan and John, who were teenagers. Mr. Hill took a cab to Wall Street in the morning, so I didn't have to get into the city early. He wanted me there at 4 p.m. so that he could do business in the car on the way back home. He would give a lift to some of the top people on Wall Street and pretty much asked them all the same questions on certain investments. Then he would come to the majority conclusion on the subject. That's the way they do business.

Wall Street

Hill was a senior partner in one of the biggest financial firms on Wall Street. They only bought and sold within the firm. Some bookkeepers received 1% of the earnings at the end of the year and still made a good living. Bonuses were good also.

The head of the company became ill, and only lasted a few months. He lived in a duplex on Park Avenue with a large home in Westchester, New York. He had it all, but his time came, which opened the door for Hill who became head of the company and was eager to change the name. Two months went by. He asked me, "is it too early to change the name of the company?" I suggested waiting at least six months, but it changed in three. Now it became time to select a senior partner, so all the partners would ask me, constantly, who is he talking about? One of the partners gave me an older Lincoln convertible for information, which I didn't give him. Finally he decided on Mr. Brown. After that, Mr. Brown wouldn't even talk to me anymore. Now he was a big shot. Mr. Hill had a nickname. It was Bunny, (what a coincidence) so we had a bunny put on the front of both Lincolns as hood ornaments. Hill didn't drive, play sports, and hardly took a vacation. He just wanted to go to Wall Street and do his thing. He was a philanthropist, because of his position on Wall Street. He could raise money at the drop of a hat.

Hill became a high-ranking official for the New York Stock Exchange and showed me the contract he signed. The underlying part, he pointed to, was no fraternizing. In his way, he now felt he could trust me and gave me a large charge account.

Hill raised money for Dick Nixon's campaign as his financial manager when he ran for president. One evening we were dropping Nixon off at his apartment. Before he left the car, he said, quote: "If I'm shot and killed while being sworn in as president, I would be the happiest man in the world." He became President in 1969 through 1974. As soon as we pulled away Hill said, "did you hear that?" I said "yes." We both agreed that becoming president was his one desire. Another day, I was driving home alone from Wall Street on the Eastside Drive. A car pulled alongside of me, it was Dick Nixon, waving and hollering "Hi Richard". I noticed one thing that the Park Avenue people would talk about all the time. That was his white shirt sleeves were always sticking out too far. If only that was the only thing that he did wrong, but there were some other things that he did that most people didn't know about. For instance he would let a high school kid interview him in his apartment, between Fifth and Madison, for their local school paper. I found out about that when he let Hill's son interview him.

Hill also raised money for John Lindsay's campaign when he ran for Mayor of New York. Most of it came from Wall Street. Hill told the Wall Street boys that Lindsay was going to be in their corner when he became Mayor. When election night came, the Hill's invited Karolee and me to the party that was being held at the Biltmore Hotel. When he won, the place went wild. It was very exciting. I enjoyed rubbing elbows with Mr. and Mrs. Hill at a social event. After that, I got to meet Mayor Lindsay at Gracie Mansion on the front steps. While congratulating him, a limo pulled up in front and the driver got out. Believe it or not, it was one of my old coaches. It was Mike Geomo. He was the heavyweight-boxing champ in the Philippines during World War II. He also worked for the sanitation department. No wonder they picked him for the Mayor's driver. Now that Lindsay was Mayor, the first thing he did when he was put into office was to hit Wall Street with a 3% transfer tax. Hill felt like crawling into a hole.

A Day With Hill

One day Hill asked me to sit with him at his desk to see what he goes through each day. I remember Hill saying to one of his buyers, if the stock goes down one sell it, I don't want any big losses, then his secretary told him that Bob Hope was on the phone. Hill looked at me and said, "Bob Hope has been after my list of money contributors and he keeps trying." The call went like this, "Hi Bob, how are you doing?" Bob Hope did a lot of talking, Hill made a lot of different faces and finally he said Bob I will contribute to any of your causes and said goodbye and hung up. Hill said, "That always stops him." The phones rang all day, wheeling and dealing. He loved it! He also took me to the dining area. They had the very best French chefs. The dining room had cathedral ceilings, and the finest woodwork. When you've got it, flaunt it!

I would pick up Hill at about the same time every day at the Exchange, parking in just about the same spot. One day I was approached by about six of New York's finest policemen, explaining to me that the mayor wanted to close the first precinct and move it to Chinatown to save money for the city. They proceeded to explain that it would mean the lack of protection in the Wall Street area, and then they asked me to please convey this to Mr. Hill for them, which I did. When Hill heard about this, he went right to town with all his connections and stopped the move. I was impressed. The only thing was, after that he would get calls from policemen who had problems. Some how they got his home phone number.

While an internal investigation was going on, the name of one of the officers who was being investigated was found on a Christmas list. The officer asked me if I could find out if Mr. Hill could help. I presented the problem to Mr. Hill. He asked if his first and last name were on the list. I said that they were, Hill replied that he couldn't help him. When I told the officer, he started crying. (He only had one year left for his retirement.) That's life in the big city.

Chapter 14: Fraternizing

The only thing that Mr. Hill and I had in common was that we both cheated. He would have me get a room for him at either the Americana or the Hilton Hotel, near the top, because none of his friends would ever go there. Money was no object. Another time Hill was invited to Washington. When he returned, he told me to get a room at the top of the Hilton Hotel, then pick up a blonde who would be wearing a full-length mink coat at LaGuardia Airport shuttle in from Washington. She will know you. I picked her up and talked with her while driving to the hotel. She was very nice. Two hours later I picked her up and drove back to LaGuardia airport and she flew back to Washington. Just like that! Another time, he asked me to get another room. I was at the hotel in the lobby; just walking out when coming in was one of his employee's wives. She saw me and turned red, turning her head so I wouldn't see her face; but I did. I felt sorry for her, how it must have been, when she saw me, to have someone know that you would belittle yourself, by having sex with your husband's boss just so that your husband could get ahead in business, but that's the Park Avenue crowd. They would do anything to get ahead. Hill told me all about it the next day.

I drove a group of Wall Street boys, looking for a neutral apartment on the East side, that they could exchange with each other. For unknown reasons, Hill, to prove that I wouldn't talk, in front of them asked me about Renaldo that I worked for. Naturally, I said, "no comment." He said, "see he won't talk." (I'm talking now…)

I also started taking pictures at this time with a Rolleiflex camera that was given to me by Karolee's father, Frank Bowman, who was the head photographer with Look

Magazine. One of his claims to fame was proving that there was a curveball in stop motion with Bob Feller pitching, in a two-page centerfold in Look magazine. When I first met Frank, he showed me a note from Ingrid Bergman and John F. Kennedy about the beautiful job he did on the cover of Look Magazine. He was shooting another cover shot with Burl Ives. He noticed the hair was growing out of Ives's nose. Frank asked him to cut it. Ives refused. Karolee's father had a fit, but Ives was tough. The hairs stayed. Bowman also received the Freedom Foundation award, but let's get back to the story. The Hill's gave me an open account at the Modern Age, which was a professional camera store. Every time Mrs. Hill had a new dress made, I would take her to Central Park and take a picture of her in it. That started me taking pictures of her whole family, which they paid me, extra for. I love this job!

Park Avenue Women

One day I was downstairs waiting for Mrs. Hill, with my camera, when I noticed this beautiful girl walking by wearing a miniskirt, Panama hat, and walking a white Russian wolfhound. What a sight! I seized the moment to say, "hold it" as I had my camera in my hand. I started taking pictures. The only thing was, I didn't have film in it. While I was taking the pictures she asked, "what it was for?" I had to think fast and replied, "springtime in New York." She agreed to let me go on. After, I asked for her phone number so that I could let her know where and when it would be in the papers. I wasn't going to use it I just had to ask. A couple of days later, I was sitting in the car waiting outside the Hill's apartment when someone knocked on the car window. It was her. She said, "you're not a photographer?" I said, "you got me." She understood and we had a good laugh. I liked that about her. We became friends. We started seeing each other, her name was Beverly. I think she just needed someone, a friend. Her husband told her it was okay for her to see me. I guess he figured I would keep her busy. This is the average young girl on Park Avenue, one who tried to take her life at least once and had a gay brother. She lived on the tenth floor overlooking Park Avenue. One time I was in front of Hill's apartment and heard a voice hollering, "Richard, Richard." I looked up, and everyone on Park Avenue did also. There she was in a mini nighty on her balcony. A picture to behold! She hollered that she would be right down. When she arrived, Mrs. Hill came out at the same time, so I introduced Beverly to her. She understood the situation, and said, "I'll take a cab." I love that woman. Beverly and I whisked away to Central Park, where we threw a blanket down that Beverly conveniently had. She began telling me about the lavish parties that she attended, where she danced all night long. At that point I asked if she would dance for me? With a little encouragement she agreed, to the sounds of a transistor radio. All this was to the envy of all the guys who passed us by. She started dancing and her moves were smooth and graceful, but very sexy. (What a life.)

Another time when I met her, she had a friend who was staying with her, an ex-Miss Sweden. Here I am, with two beauties standing on the corner of Park Avenue, trying to figure out where and what we were going to do and believe it or not, the young debutant walked by, that's the one that couldn't ask me herself to stop for a drink. What did she think? We decided that we would go to the Four Seasons restaurant for lunch. Here I am with two beauties in a great place, which gave me a feeling in the pit of my stomach that I loved. I think the feeling was "look at me." During that time, Miss Sweden told a story that she was at a party with the

Beatles in Europe, where they cut a record by the name of "All You Need Is Love",. That must have been fun.   I found out later, she became a lesbian. So much for life's trends. Beverly took Don Ryan, my basketball buddy, and me out to lunch at the Plaza Hotel. I guess to show off. It was perfect. When the bill came and she gave the waitress the credit card, the waitress came back and said the card wasn't any good. You talk about a Park Avenue, spoiled brat, attacking the waitress! This was a sight to see. Don and I could hardly keep from laughing. This was supposed to be our high society lunch experience. What it ended up to be was pure chaos. Beverly huffed and puffed and took us across the street to the Playboy club. We finally had a nice time after we paid the bills.

One day she told me she and her husband were moving to another apartment on upper Fifth Avenue. After the move, she took me up to see it. I couldn't believe it.   It had metal floors with bolts. I wondered what the neighbors thought when she walked across the floor with high heels? Campbell Soup boxes and Marilyn Monroe pictures were all around. I guess that's modern. With the new apartment, she wanted to change. The end came when she said to me as I was lying on her, that she was turning over a new leaf. Well, how about that? That was the end of the relationship.

Joan

Hill's daughter, Joan, wanted to learn how to drive so I would take her up to the Century Country Club parking lot in Westchester, where there was plenty of room. As I got out of the car to go around to the other side, Joan got behind the wheel and drove off into traffic. I almost had a heart attack just standing there waiting. She was a handful. When she finally came back I sent her to driving school. Joan also wanted to model with her height and looks she could.

She was only 16 but looked 18. We did a test shooting in Central Park, walking together, which sold to Omega Watch Company. We were head to head as lovers. It was her first job. She also liked to go to the beach. I had to take her as her protector. She was a tease. I took a lot of pictures of her in the park. Another of her favorites was to go bouncing around town with Don Ryan and me. I guessed she felt safe with us. Now it came time to find a car for Joan. She picked out a red GTO from one of my Killeen's friends known as Superman. He gave me a kickback from the sale. I told Mrs. Hill, she thought that was great. I love that woman. Joan was showing off to me on how she could park in front of the Park Avenue apartment. It was a busy street. While she was backing into the spot, the front end was turning out. A truck came along and knocked the front left light off. What an embarrassing way to learn. I couldn't stop laughing. Another time Joan and I went to the movies together on 3rd Avenue and 70th street. It was a full house. In the middle of the movie, smoke started coming out of all of the upper vents. People started running, out of control. I told Joan just to stay seated. The smoke was still above us. Most of the people were out of the theater by then. We started walking out slowly. The fire trucks were just pulling up. All the people were outside looking at the entrance. We walked out of the smoke. The people started cheering, Joan thought that was real cool. I did too. (Maybe dumb.)

John

John Hill was a good kid. He was a sharp dresser. He looked like Rudolph Valentino, if you remember him. He liked to go bouncing with Don and me also, drinking around town.

One night it was freezing and I had to go to the bathroom. We started looking for a place, when I spotted this little bar on a side street. In we went. It was crowded. The bartender knew me and asked if I would sign his basketball. His name was Art Haymen, an ex New York Knick, who had put on a little weight. I hardly recognized him. John was impressed. A girl came up to me and was very forward. I grabbed her chest, and that turned her away. I had had a few too many. That was one of John's nights out with me. John was attending Rollins College in Winter Park, Florida. The family had bought him a new Cutlass for his birthday. They had me drive the new car to him in Florida, which gave us another opportunity to start partying. I felt like I was back at Playboy. John's next school was Winchendon College in Massachusetts. Mr. Hill had a library built for the college to get him in. When John graduated, Joan and I went to the graduation. The family couldn't make it. Now we were trying to figure out who I was going to be. We settled on a friend of the family, it went well. After graduation, some of the kids who graduated with John, lived along the way back to New York City so we drove them home also. When we stopped for gas and opened the back door, all the beer cans poured out onto the ground. That Lincoln will never smell the same. We dropped off one of the boys at his home estate. His family owned one of the biscuit companies. They had a 100-foot yacht at their dock that we boarded. I asked a stupid question; the question was "how much does one of these things cost"?

John's father, Mr. Hill, wanted John to follow him in Wall Street, which John didn't like. He ended up going to LA and starting a clothing line. It was very successful. I'm sure that his father backed him. He was a good kid.

Susan Hill

She did all kinds of charity work. One was working with the children with serious health conditions, which she finally had to leave because it was too heart breaking. She quickly turned to The Home For The Aged because it was less stressful. Working for her was like working for royalty. We used to sing our favorite song. "I say tomayto you say tomahto." She was also on the board of Lincoln Center and would attend most of the performances. If she couldn't make one, she would let me go in her place. I would attend; leaving the limo in front, taking advantage of everything I could, even taking the best seat in the house. It made me feel like anyone I wanted to be. It's a world of make-believe.

Trust was very important. She would show me the hiding place for all her expensive jewelry. She also showed me a building that her grandfather gave her. It was a whole city block in the upper 80's on the East side. They made me feel trusted.

Chapter 15: A Friend of the Hills

Mr. Cook made a large investment and was sure that this deal would go through. Naturally, it didn't. It affected Mr. Cook mentally, so that he thought he was a King and totally out of control. They put him into a private sanitarium upstate New York. The Hill's thought it would be nice to buy him a present and have me deliver it. I drove up in this new black Lincoln, wearing my black suit and tie, finally arriving at the hospital front gate. The guard waved at me as I passed through. There were several buildings, they all looked alike. I selected one. I rang the bell and a nurse came to the door and said, "hello doctor." I went along with it. It happened to be the right building. She showed me to Mr. Cook's room and let me in. It was like a hotel, very large and comfortable. I began a conversation and gave Mr. Cook his present, which was a tape recorder. After about 15 minutes of conversation, the door opened. A gentleman looked in and beckoned to me with his finger to come out. When I came out of the room, he said, "who are you?" I explained who I was. He said Mr. Cook is not supposed to have any visitors or presents. He had to go back into the room and retrieve the present. I did look like a doctor. I remember when Mrs. Hill was in Lenex Hill Hospital. I had no problem getting in. The nurses would all call me Doctor. I had no problem. Mr. Cook is out now and doing well.

Country Club

Century Country Club was one of the most exclusive clubs in Westchester. There I met a lot of high society women who would come up to my car and start chatting with me. One day, Mr. Hill told me to deliver a package to Mary at her home in Westchester. This was on a Saturday, which I normally didn't work. He said she would be expecting me. I understood. I drove up to the grand mansion and knocked on the door. No one answered. I was just about to get into the car, when the front door opened. The maid called to me and said that Ms. Mary would be ready to see me in 10 minutes. The maid then made me breakfast, and I listened to a talking dog. Mary finally came down. She looked beautiful. I was used to seeing her in golf clothes at the club. She said, how very sorry she was for oversleeping, but wanted to show me the house and grounds. They were breathtaking. Now to get onto the reason why I was there. The conversation was light, going through my mind was how do you ask a high society woman out? I knew that she liked me, that was good, but how and when do you make your move to ask her? (Without looking like a jerk.) She went on about the house, and material things she had that made it even harder for me. It might look like I was just after her, because of her wealth. Maybe, I was, but I'm here because she wants me here. That's why. Finally, an opening occurred when she started talking about food and a great place for lunch in town (thank God). Cool like-I asked her if she would like to go there for lunch, she responded that she would love it. I still think Mary manipulated me for lunch. She told me that her husband went one way and she the other. I didn't even know she was married, but her looks overpowered my judgment. At lunch, she said to me, "do you like me," in a shy way? I gritted my teeth and figured what the hell. My answer to that was, if liking you is that I want to grab you, kiss you, throw you on a bed and make passionate love to you all night, then I like you. She took a deep breath and gave me a hug. (So the affair began...) We dated for a couple of months wondering where this thing was going to take us, but like it should be, the novelty wore off; but it was fun.

Vacation

Mr. and Mrs. Hill finally went on a vacation to a small island in South America. While they were on the beach alone, two other people approached them through the heat of the rising mist of the beach. It was the Governor and Mrs. Rockefeller of New York. What a coincidence. They had a couple of days together to talk. Hill was a Port Authority commissioner and loved to get through town as fast as possible, even if it meant going up onto sidewalks and through red lights. The result was four Port Authority State of New York emblems for both cars. I used these cars to commute to New Jersey through the Lincoln Tunnel. All the Port Authority police would salute me, thinking I was the Commissioner, and the police treated me like a diplomat. I loved it!

115

Port Authority

The Port Authority wanted to build a new airport in New Jersey on the Atlantic shoreline, offering the people more than what the property and homes were worth, but the people and the communities wouldn't go for it and turned down the offer. Hill and the Port Authority could not believe that they would turn this deal down, but it goes to show you how little they know about the common people; not taking into consideration that these people had been living in these homes for years and years. Their children would probably live there also. It's like the government. They don't know how the other half-lives.

The 21 Club

Hill liked the 21 Club and met a lot of celebrities, some of whom he introduced me to, for instance; Vice President Agnew. He had made some ethnic remarks about Jews. Agnew called Hill to get together all the top Jewish businessmen, to meet at the 21 Club where Agnew apologized to them. After they finished, Hill brought Agnew over and introduced him to me. That made me feel like I had some importance.

When The Lights Went Out In New York City

I was sitting in the car on 5th Avenue, next to Mount Sinai Hospital, waiting for Mr. Hill. He was on the board of the hospital. I was looking out over Central Park to the west side. Suddenly, all the lights went out. The generators in the hospital started and smoke came from the chimneys. Hill came running out to the car. We started back to 72nd Street and Park Avenue. All the stoplights were out and all the traffic was on it's own. We parked and walked up to the fourth floor of his apartment building. I went back to the kitchen where all the cooks and maids were sitting around with candles aglow. I suggested we play cards. We ended up playing and drinking most of the night until we all fell asleep. That's where I was when the lights went out in New York City.

Chapter 16: A Little Affair

I had an affair with this little blonde who I met in my visits back to Killeen's tavern. She lived in Brooklyn and was under the impression that I was going to leave my wife for her. I guess we have all heard that story before? One night I was trying to make time after leaving her, crossing Manhattan to New Jersey. I was heading across town on 57th street approaching 3rd Avenue, in Hill's brand new Lincoln. A car had its blinkers on waiting to make a left turn just ahead of me. I had the light, when, all of a sudden, he started to make his turn. A head-on collision occurred. My hands that held the steering wheel hit the dashboard at impact. No seatbelts in those days. The two cars were stuck together, and the passengers in the other car jumped out. While the driver was putting the car in reverse, the two others were jumping on the hood trying to dislodge their vehicle from mine. Then there was a tap on my passenger side window. I opened it. A gay voice asked me if I was okay? I nodded yes, thinking it would be better if I stayed in the car. Obviously, there was something wrong with the other vehicle. They were trying to get away. The gay guy asked if I wanted a drink? I just said okay. He ran off. They were still jumping on the hood, burning rubber in reverse, trying to get the two cars apart to no avail. The gay guy appeared at the window with a scotch and soda and handed it to me. I took the drink, the police arrived, and here I was with a drink in my hand. I opened the drivers side window and the policeman said, "what happened Rich?" Thank heaven, he knew me. He said he could see what happened and would take care of everything. I asked him if he would have the car towed to the Lincoln dealer on 11th Avenue. He said "no problem." It's just great to know people in New York City. I took a cab up to 73rd street, hopped into the other Lincoln and went home. How about that?

Fishing Trip, New York's Sacandaga Reservoir

I had a craving for an outdoor experience after I read about a record pike being caught before the freeze in the Sacandaga Reservoir, located in upper New York State. I decided I was going to try for that record. I had a rowboat with a 6-horse power Johnson motor on it. My boss, Hill, thought I was crazy, but gave me a bottle of 20-year-old brandy, because the temperature was dropping that weekend. I even lowered the passenger seat in my car, so I could sleep in the car if necessary. Blankets, fishing equipment and coolers filled with food and drink were loaded in the car. I drove up the New York Thruway to the Adirondacks. I picked a waterway by a bridge that led to the Reservoir. I slept in the car overnight. Early in the morning it was cold, so I made coffee, pulled the boat off the top of the car, and found there was several feet of ice starting to build from the shoreline out. I broke through the ice and it seemed to be getting colder, with stronger winds. When I stirred my coffee that I had made with a sterno, my plastic spoon melted. I took a picture of the spoon and ice on the shoreline with my camera. I loaded the boat and the little 6hp engine that started right up. I greased my face. The boots I wore would have taken me down like an anchor if I ever turned over, but I took that chance. I put a line in and started trolling, thinking I had a chance of catching my record fish. Everything was going fine until the engine started missing and then finally quit. The wind was blowing harder and the temperature was still dropping. It finally blew me to an island. I took a picture of the boat being swamped on the shore. The only thing I could do was to pull the boat to the other side of the island and let the wind blow me to the mainland, so I did. I landed on a closed up nudist camp. I pulled the boat up on shore and tied it up. Now, I had to start walking back to the car, about 4 miles over the bridge, to the beach where the car was parked. Thank God, when I got there it started. I drove back to the boat on the beach and pulled up alongside it. All of a sudden the rear right tire fell into a hole on the beach. It was getting late and colder. I started digging, working up a sweat. I finally gave up. I knew I had to change clothes and get warm for the night. I took some pictures and started the car to get some heat going. I had extra blankets so I put them across the windows. I changed clothes, turned off the car and slept, exhausted, all night. In the morning there was a foot of snow on the ground. I remembered seeing a gas station by the bridge, so I started walking another 4 miles with blisters on my feet from the boots. I made it to the station. I was so lucky, (ha!) because the station owner had just gotten a new tow truck. On the way to the car and boat I told him my story. When we arrived at the car he stayed back from the beach. He had plenty of line to reach the car and pulled it out like a feather. I was so grateful. I asked how much? He said, "Buddy after what you've been through, give me 20 bucks and call it even." I was so happy to get back to the city with my fishing story and pictures to prove what happened. I don't know where the pictures are now but they are very clear in my memory. It was an experience I will never forget.

A Meeting On Route 3

I was leaving the city one evening, after a hot summer day. The buildings were acting like heaters, holding on to the heat of the day. I decided to put the top down before I went through the Lincoln Tunnel. When I arrived on the New Jersey side, the temperature dropped 15 degrees. A car passed me on my right. A nice-looking girl was driving. I moved up to be next to her. She smiled. I motioned her to move over to the side of the road, which she did. She parked behind me. I went back to her car and joined her. We talked. It led to our necking until a cop stopped and told us to move. The second time he came around, we had to move. I asked where she lived. She looked across Route 3 and pointed to the Peter Pan Motel, (oh brother). We drove over. As we were going into her room, the manager started hollering at us. She told me not to listen to him at that point. I didn't care, as I was ready for her. She was obviously the motel's prostitute. We entered the room, which was in disarray. But who cared? She told me to get into the bed. I quickly disrobed, waiting for her. She finally arrived, turning the lights out, which I thought was different than what I was used to.

Then she began slowly starting to give me a tongue bath. It was my first. I touched her breasts as she was crawling on me. I could feel that her skin had been burnt. You know that dry slick feeling; a quick thought went through my mind. Had she been tortured at one time or something like that? We went on and after we finished, she started talking about dating and starting a relationship. I felt sorry for her. I figured she was going to be stuck in this life forever. Life can be a bitch! On my way home, as my mind started clearing, I thought about how many guys had slept in that bed. I started speeding up and couldn't wait to brush my teeth and get into the shower. What a weird experience.

JOAN

One of Joan Hill's boyfriends sent Mr. Hill a case of Dewar's, which was his favorite drink; but it still pissed him off.

He told me to return it and tell him never to see his daughter again, or else. I agreed to do it, thinking oh boy now I'm a muscle man. This guy lived in the Village, in a dumpy area. I rang the bell. He was home, "damn it". I returned the booze and gave him the message. We never heard from him again after that. Without my knowledge, Joan received some threatening phone calls. Mrs. Hill had the phone tapped, which I didn't know. I was making calls to the Hilton Hotel, on behalf of Mr. Hill, arranging for rooms, which he told me not to do from his home. I was too lazy to go there and do it in person. Because of the tapped phones, Mrs. Hill found out about what was going on, and subsequently divorce proceedings were started. I certainly learned from that experience. I felt bad about having to leave Hill's family. I had grown to love the family, which I told Mrs. Hill, but it came back to me from the cook, Elaina, that I said I loved Mrs. Hill; but maybe I really did after thinking about it. It was time to move on.

Karolee Goes To Work

Back at home; Karolee decided that she wanted to go back to work as a waitress and barmaid. I always thought she would get bored just being at home. She loved to talk. I didn't live and learn. I had to quit the Parks and Recreation job, so I could be with the girls at night. Karolee began staying out later and later. The gentleman who Karolee worked for threw a party for the whole staff and their families at his home. When I met him, I could see in his eyes how embarrassed he was to meet our girls and me. I just knew that there was something going on between them. I'm finding that all my cheating is coming back to haunt me. It's funny how the male mind works. When she started cheating, that may just be in my mind, I'm upset. I feel this is the beginning of the end. I made a promise to myself that I would give this marriage one more year and would try my best to hold it together. Sadly, nothing changed within the year that I had given myself. One morning I made breakfast for Karolee and the girls. I told her I was leaving and that I couldn't take it any longer. She was surprised. I left with my clothes and my trophies again.

Karolee got a lawyer. We started going through the procedure. We were told to go to counseling as a last resort, but it wasn't working. The last time we went to counseling, as we were leaving, with my hand on the doorknob, Karolee asked if I wanted to come back to the house? It's funny how things change when you're separated for a while. I turned towards her, my heart bursting with joy, walking towards her with my arms open saying, "yes, yes!" When she said that she would leave, I stepped back and gulped. The feeling of joy turned to heartbreak and weakness. I couldn't say anything. I just had to get out of there. I gave her the house, agreed to child support and left.

Karolee's new boyfriend moved into the house right away. I lost 15 pounds just thinking and worrying about my girls. I guess I really screwed up! God knows what the boyfriend was like. Just the thought of someone else being with her sent me into a jealous rage, thinking of all kinds of sexual things that they would be doing. I had this feeling in the pit of my stomach that was making me sick. Looking at me from someone else's point of view, I was someone who they would feel sorry for.

The Mind - Divorce # 2 (1978)

I just couldn't stop thinking about her, as hard as I would try. It would take a long time before this feeling would go away. Did I do the right thing? I moved into an apartment, in New Jersey. Now I had to start taking care of myself, not knowing anything about cooking. I decided to make salads to keep myself in shape, so I made my trip to the local grocery store where I didn't know the difference between cabbage and lettuce. While browsing around in confusion, the women in the area knew I was in trouble. They began helping me in different ways of preparing salads. I felt great with all the attention that I was getting at this time. Maybe this isn't so bad.

But reality sets in. When I was with a girl, the only thing I could talk about uncontrollably was my breakup. I kept telling myself that I wouldn't, but I couldn't stop. I even went to Karolee's business to watch her. It was killing me. All the tunes that were popular at that time stuck in my mind, like "She's Got Lying Eyes," by the Eagles and "How Long Has This Been Going On" by Ace. This was the most miserable time of my life, but I guess I deserved it. I still loved her, but time heals all wounds, (they say). So here I go, leaving with the song "Baby Don't Leave Me This Way"! (By: Thelma Houston)

I'm alone now; I will never find another like her. I'm willing to forgive her for everything she did to me, if she would only take me back; but will she forgive me? It's funny; I cheated on her for a long time, but when I found out that she cheated on me, I was totally devastated. Who the hell do I think I am? I love her and was willing to leave because she hurt me. In my mind I guess she belittled me, but that's the way we are. (Live and learn.)

Trying To Start Again

I got a job with Stern's Auto Center on Route 3, New Jersey, as an assistant manager. While working at the Center, I was still reacting to my divorce, and talked about it constantly. I was not in a good mood either. I would meet lots of women who came in to have their cars worked on. One woman invited me to a party for singles in Westchester, New York. When I arrived, it was like a lamb being led to the slaughter. The women had all gone through a divorce; of course they got everything, including the gold fixtures. The women outnumbered the men four to one. One of the women asked me how long I'd been on the circuit. This was a new language to me. I'm still learning. I believe that some things in life happen for a reason. Maybe things are even pre-ordained in a way. Going through all these ups and downs is the only way you can fulfill life. I've known a lot of lives that are stagnant, unfulfilled, and just a waste. Doing a variety of things is the only way to live, at least for me. So that led me to decide to take Lisa, my 12-year-old daughter, on an adventure to Florida. I had just bought an old TR 6 Triumph, and not knowing the condition it was in, we took off and just hit the road.

Everything was going well until we approached Georgia. I told Lisa to watch the heat gauge and if it moves let me know. Sure as anything, Lisa yelled out, "it's moving." Yes, it's overheating. We moved to the side of I-95, letting the engine cool off and started again. We were only 20 miles from Augusta, Georgia. We coasted in and found a dealer, where they had one water pump in stock. It was easy to put on. I let Lisa tighten the last few bolts and took a picture of her filling it with water, we were on our way again. We arrived in Fort Lauderdale, where we took in the boats and the beaches. We were heading back north when our starter went. That's when I taught Lisa how to pop the clutch. That wasn't so bad until the clutch went. We stopped at a dealer and they gave us a price that we couldn't afford. They also said that we wouldn't make it back to New York, but we tried anyway, popping the clutch, throwing it into third gear. Lisa was trying different beaches out and rating them. She decided the Boca Raton Beach was the best. We were moving along nicely as we approached Jacksonville. Lisa wanted to check out the beach. That meant getting off I-95 going east and hitting traffic, but she wanted to do it, so we did. I remember getting into the beach parking and made sure that we parked on a hill so it would make it easier for starting. Lisa gave the beach a bad rating. Once we got rolling we were on our way and we made it back to New York. It was a great and exciting adventure that we will never forget. I had the TR 6 repaired.

Chapter 17: Moving To Florida

I was modeling part-time for an agency by the name of Serendipity. Mil-jean was the owner. She had two offices, one in New York City and the other in New Jersey. Karolee did some modeling for her also. I called in one day to find out if any checks had come in for me. Mil-jean answered the phone, and we talked a little. She told me that she was getting a divorce. I told her the best thing to do was to keep busy, learning from my past experiences. I suggested that we go out for dinner, she accepted the invitation. She called Karolee and asked if it was all right that the two of us went out. Karolee had no problem with it. Mil-jean was having a hard time with her divorce, so she decided to sell both of her agencies and move to Florida. That's where her parents lived. She asked me if I wanted to move with her. I thought I loved the weather and this trip should be smoother then with Lisa. I thought, nothing ventured nothing gained, so I agreed. We left for Florida during the gas shortage. The weather was in the teens and we waited for a half hour for gas. We announced over our ham set, which most people had in those days, that we were on our way to Florida. The return from everyone listening was good luck, have a great trip, go for it, I wish I could go with you. Off we went towing the TR 6 with a Mercury Cougar.

We got lucky in Washington, getting gas rather quickly. Next up was South Carolina. They didn't even experience the gas shortage. As we reached Florida, driving through Jacksonville, the temperature was 27°. What happened to Florida?

We finally arrived at Highland Beach, Florida, which is just east of Boca Raton on the ocean. That's where Mil-jean's family lived. I never felt comfortable living with Mil-jean's parents. They always made me feel like a leech. I guess, as a parent, I would feel the same.

Old Boca Raton

Her parent's home was on a little island called Bell Lebo. The front of the house looked out into the Intracoastal Waterway the rear looked onto a bay with docks and boats. I always had a low heartbeat in the 40s, like I was in hibernation. This was because of my large heart due to sports. One night, about 1 a.m. in the morning I was sound asleep.   Mil-jean's son came into the room, shaking me with a hysterical voice, telling me there was someone outside the back window. That sudden disturbance threw my heart out of rhythm. (Which I will get back to later.) The noise outside was the local police. It seems the boat that was docked across the bay from our back window was sitting well below the water line, which means that there was a heavy load of something in it. The police were keeping an eye on it. Finally, that next night, the homeowner came out and started unloading the boat. It was loaded with bales of marijuana. One of the local policemen was an ex-New Jersey cop, and always wanted to say, "This is a bust!" He got the opportunity of saying just that and caught them flat-footed.

Problems

Now to get back to my heart problem… I went to the local doctor. He was a new doctor and asked me if I had any problems with my left arm? I said sometimes. He told me that he wanted me to go to Dr. Zachariah Zachariah, one of the top heart doctors in Fort Lauderdale. He told me that I should have a catheterization. I didn't know what that was, in those days. It was a risky procedure. I was rolled into the operating room, which was like a freezer. They were putting things up my groin. I looked at a wire going up through my heart on a TV screen. Then they told me to get ready. We are going to put dye into your heart. That's so that they could see the blood passing through the small vessels. It raised my temperature sky-high. Then it was over. Back in my recovery room, I had a beautiful view overlooking the Atlantic Ocean. While meditating, I was interrupted by the TV describing the launching of the Space Shuttle Challenger that had just exploded. Minutes later, through my window, I could see the smoke from the disaster floating south, passing my window like a black storm-cloud, holding the memories of all those who it took in 1986. (I'll never forget it). The doctor said I had the heart of a 20-year-old. That was good news, but it took months before my heart smoothed out again. I wonder if all that was necessary?

Drugs

Mil-Jean and I started looking for a house. We found one on the Intracoastal in Boca Raton that was being rented and still had a month to go. We couldn't wait and started to do some gardening in the front of the house. Terry, the gentleman who was renting the house, had a 35-foot cigarette boat at the dock. The police were sure that he was running drugs. They were collecting his garbage and checking out the vacuum bags. They did find remnants of marijuana, but still had to catch him in the act. He got nervous because we were around a lot. He took off with his boat. Since he was gone, I opened the garage door and found blankets over the window and a sophisticated scale. He also left a dining room set, a Sony TV and workout materials. We moved in. After about a month, Terry knocked on the door, late one evening. He collected the scale, the weights and the TV. That's all he wanted. He left us the dinning room set. It was the time of drugs.

One of my other neighbors bid on boats that were confiscated in drug busts. One was a 55' Hatteras with a full load of marijuana that was spotted in the ocean. When the sun reflected on the glass sliding doors to the cabin, the Coast Guard boat saw the reflection and decided to investigate it. The Hatteras crew saw the Coast Guard coming, so they poured gas all over the bales of marijuana. With the lifeboat in the water, they shot a flare gun into the open doors. The flare bounced all over and landed into a small sink, (bad break). The Coast Guard arrived and that was that! My neighbor had pictures of all the bales unloaded on the dock and he ended up buying the Hatteras. Welcome to early Boca Raton!

Boca House

Mil-jean started working for the Sun Sentinel and Ft. Lauderdale News as a fashion and beauty editor. She also began a syndicated column called, "Ask Mil-jean". She got them to do a full-page picture story about me with Playboy. Somehow that seemed newsworthy.

The article included a picture that had a Playboy Bunny sitting next to me. Actually, it was a Bunny doll. The

128

magazine would also sponsor our trips to different retirement homes at Christmas time; I would dress as Santa Claus and Miljean would dress as Mrs. Claus. We would enter each home with presents and were received happily by families and patients. One room that I entered had a gentleman who was in a coma for months. The whole family was in the room also. I leaned over handing him a present and wishing him a Merry Christmas. As we were leaving the room, the wife came out with tears in her eyes, saying; he smiled, he smiled. (Even if it was true or not.) It was very gratifying. The news media heard about it and tracked us down. Miljean did most of the talking, because I had so much hair in my mouth. It was on TV the next day.

Chapter 18: Meeting My Best Friends

The house Mil-jean and I purchased was everything that I ever wanted. It was on the Intracoastal with a dock and a pool. One day we decided to take a boat ride in a rowboat with a little outboard motor on it. The sun was strong and bright. I decided to put a beach umbrella in the hole in the middle seat to keep the sun off Mil-jean. We started down the Intracoastal, I must admit, we looked rather funny. Mil-jean was wearing a bikini bathing suit, which drew a lot of attention. Boats were passing by, turning around taking pictures and waving at us. We finally pulled into Spanish River Park. There was no room at the dock, so we pulled the boat up onto the beach. Everyone was looking at us as we looked out of place in this tiny boat.

A couple that was parked on the beach next to us introduced themselves. It was Dick and Milly Olson. Dick was a large man with a scruffy beard and Milly, with a white two-piece bathing suit, looked great. They were in the process of building a large house on the Intracoastal and asked if we wanted to see it? Of course we did, although it was in the beginning stages of construction, with just the foundation. I told them I knew something about electrical work from my father. Dick asked if I would like to work for him on the house. I knew that my experience working with my father would help me one day. I like working with my hands, and it was like going to school. We called it the Olson School of Electric Contracting. When I started working there, I was enthusiastic

and would get to the site early, eager to get things done. When Dick and Milly arrived, they would suggest going out for breakfast. Off we went. Afterward we would work for a couple of hours then Dick would suggest going to lunch. It ended up to be lots of fun and no pressure at all. They became my best friends.

I sold my sports car to buy a Ford Taurus station wagon that I could use for work. Everything was going fine until…

Lucky fall

One day, while I was working on the house alone, I was attempting to put up a tongue and groove board in the upper ceiling of the second floor walkway, with my hands over my head trying to fit the grooves. I slid the ladder under me to a new position. All of a sudden, the one leg slipped off the deck. I was starting to fall. It seemed to be in slow motion, hitting my shoulder on the second-floor ledge, falling between a Bobcat and cement mixer, finally landing on my back. The ground was sandy, thank God. I didn't realize at that moment that I had driven my left foot into the ground, which also helped cushion the fall. I lay there for a few minutes realizing how lucky I was that I didn't hit any of the equipment. I tried to shake it off and went back up and finished the ceiling. My left ankle started swelling, I drove to the hospital. My ankle was x-rayed. A slight fracture was found. I think I was very lucky. Dick and Milly were very upset. I can just imagine how they felt, but I guess it's all part of the job.

After two years and 200 miles of wiring to accommodate a four-story redwood house. I found that this was the occupation for me, getting so much satisfaction and accomplishing something I loved doing. I decided to go out on my own. I got the necessary licenses and started my own business as a handyman. My big start was when I put my cards in all the mailboxes at a condo development on Highland Beach, which consisted of 270 apartments. After I did that, the manager got wind of it. He took me aside and told me that soliciting was not allowed. I assured him I would never do it again, however, people started calling. My specialty ended up being kitchen ceilings and lighting. They called them Signature Ceilings. The residents wanted me to do most of the work in their apartments. Trust was

most important and they knew they could trust me. Even the condo association had me do all their work. The business expanded to other condos.

Marriage #3

Mil-jean and I finally decided to get married in our local church by Pastor Dingle. We did things for the church. I coached the basketball team, and Mil-jean gave beauty classes. The church was expanding. They bought the Greek Church next door, built a gymnasium and a home for the aged; just like a big business would expand. The church had meetings to raise money for their expansion. At one of these meetings, the gentleman from the podium announced that Dr. Smith gave $10,000. How did that make the parishioners feel? The poor guys who used to give two dollars on Sundays now had to give five. They had church people come to your home and tried to get 10% of your income. Why is the church expanding so much $$?

During that time, Mil-Jean started a TV show on fashion and beauty. The newspaper didn't like it. They saw it as a conflict of interest. Being an aggressive woman, she then started her own magazine named Boca Life. We were invited to every event in Boca. I started to like wearing a tux and acting the part. We even did the restaurant culinary testing. I actually wrote a column on golf. I would play a golf course and write about it. Mil-jean did all the editing, as my writing needed it. Mil-jean became friends with Lynda Carter, you know-Wonder Woman. She had put her picture on the cover of Boca Life magazine. It is an interesting reflection, as my ex-wife, Karolee, doubled for Lynda Carter in parades, wearing the Wonder Woman outfit.

Celebrity Tennis Tournament

The Junior League ran a fundraising tournament and dinner. I got to meet all of the celebrities who attended. When the magazine, Boca Life, covered the event. I was the photographer this time. There were all sorts of TV people like Mary Hart, Lorne Green, some "Mash people", "Candid Camera people," and others. It was the celebrities against the non-celebrities in a tennis tournament. It started an argument between Lorne Green and his wife. Green's wife said she was a celebrity, but Lorne disagreed. I'm not sure it was ever settled. I didn't think she was. At dinner that night we interviewed all the celebrities and were very impressed with their congeniality.

Back To Work

A decorator called me for a job in Highland Beach. It was a new building penthouse on the seventieth floor. She explained that her client was a male and all the bathrooms were already in pink tile. He wanted them changed to black. Sledgehammers were used to break up all of the tubs, tiles, and floors. It was a shame. The toilets were the only salvageable things. We sold them. I finally got to meet Ron Mick, the owner. When we found out that we both came from Astoria, Queens, New York; we became good friends. Ron proceeded to tell me that he went to NYU and graduated with Governor Mario Cuomo who was preparing to run for president the following year. One of the rooms in the penthouse was going to be used by Cuomo so the Secret Service checked the place out six months in advance of his coming. (That was exciting.)

Ron wanted a lap pool and grass. I needed more help so I hired two more men, John Cooke and Rick Sheridan, who became good friends of mine. Rick was a good-looking guy who could have any girl he wanted. He was a hard-worker.

To get in touch with him I had to let the phone ring six times. That would give him the time he needed to run down the stairs to get to the phone booth that was out on the street below his apartment. That worked out just fine for a year until the phone booth was taken away. Now what? Rick, John and I discovered a mutual love of the game of golf. We spent much time together, playing the game.

Ron, the man we were working for, had recently been divorced and had a bout with cancer. He seemed to have beat it. He and I would stand on the penthouse roof overlooking the Atlantic Ocean. He would say, "when this is all finished, we'll take all the guys out on my new boat to the islands and party." (It seemed as though he was trying to make up for lost time.)

One day I got a call from Ron. He wanted me to come over to the apartment where he was staying. He was in the diamond business and other things in China. He wanted me to meet a business associate who had just arrived from China. The associate was a Chinese woman whom he said was worth hundreds of millions. When I arrived, she was in the back room. Ron called to her to come out and meet me. She was wearing a peacock gown. She looked like a princess. I didn't know whether to kiss her hand or bow. Then she said, clearly with her Chinese accent, 'would you like some coffee?" (Well, I'll be damned!) Ron was later told that his cancer had returned. That really hurts. You have all these plans, and you know your time is limited. Shortly after that he was gone. Life can be a bitch. He was a good man, and I liked him. It was hard to take.

Psychic

Mil-Jean and I were on the beach in Boca, soaking in the sun. Suddenly, she sat up quickly and said there's something wrong. We had to get home as quick as possible (I said to myself. Now, what?) Sure enough, Mil-jean's daughter had fallen off her bike and broken her wrist. I always knew Miljean was a witch! She used to tell me a story about a UFO that hovered over her head in New Jersey one night. I guess that could do funny things to you. She wasn't afraid to start new projects, like the National Models Convention that we had every year in July. We rented the Boca Raton Hotel for three days. All the top agencies were there to find new models. The aspiring models came from all over the United States and Canada. We had Bert Parks, one year, as our Master of Ceremonies. When he came into the hotel I introduced myself to him. I said, "Mr. Parks, I'm Richard Bennett." His response was: "Of course you are! Nice to meet you." The guy was a pro; he knew just what to do at the closing show without even telling him what we wanted.

Lisa, my daughter, came down from New York to help out. She was 16 years old at that time. The agencies were very interested in her. She, on the other hand, had no interest in modeling. "I'm just helping my father," was her typical response to their inquiries. I guess with her mother and father both being models, it was not something she wanted to do.

Two years later, however, she changed her mind and decided to try the business. She did well modeling all over Europe. One of her jobs sent her to Italy. While there, she picked up another job that was to be shot in Cuba. She flew in on Soviet Airline. The plane looked like it was stripped down to make it lighter. When she arrived, she posed for bathing suit shots on the beach with horses; which she loved. After a couple of days of shooting, she finished the job and asked if she could ride the horse on the beach. The director gave her the okay. As she was enjoying the ride down the beach, she looked up to the dunes and saw soldiers with guns. She wasn't sure just what to do, so, she waved at them and when they waved back she felt she was all right and returned to the site.

Shortly after, she decided that she was so close to the states that she would visit me in Florida. She called, telling me that she would fly into Miami on a prop plane from Cuba. Somehow she got by customs with two boxes of unopened Havana cigars. Beauty opens lots of doors. I picked her up and we tried to do everything in her two-day stay before she had to fly to New York and back to Italy. We decided that we both loved fishing, so we gave it a go. I had a 25-foot inboard Sea Ray, which we took to the Boca Raton Inlet, where the waves were breaking over the sea walls. I told her it didn't look favorable. Just then a 35-foot boat came by us and went out. Lisa looked at me and said: "Well!"

We decided to do the same, "oh brother!" Here we go. The seas were 6 feet. We crashed through the inlet waves and finally got out. I told Lisa to hold the wheel and head straight out into the waves. I started letting the line out with frozen ballyhoo for bait. I didn't even get the line out 20 yards, when I had a hit. It was a bull dolphin, the biggest I've ever seen. I wanted a picture of it before we lost him so Lisa let go of the wheel and attempted to take some pictures. While getting the shots of the fish, the boat turned, and she slipped into the bait well, scratching her shin. It was a pretty good gash, but being a trooper, she said, "let's get him in." Somehow we managed to get the fish in the boat. Lisa wanted to catch another one, which she did. We then made it back safely. However, she lost jobs because of the scratch on her shin. She always tells the story that the fish bit her. It was a 25-pound bull dolphin.

Killeen's

Bobby, the brat, was part of the Killeen's crowd back in
New York. He was a runner for
Gotti, doing whatever he was
told. Much of it was illegal and
he got caught. He wouldn't talk
and was given two years in the
clink. When he was released,
a coming out party was given at
the Elks club on Queens
Boulevard, New York.
Everyone was there. I drove
up from Florida to attend. No
cameras were allowed. Danny Doyle was the master of
ceremonies, of course there were strippers; the whole works.
You could tell who was who by the way they dressed. Danny
took me around to meet some of the old faces that I did not
recognize. One of the black suited guys said to me: "We
used to bet on most of your games." If I had known that then I
probably would have choked. I owe Bobby a favor. There
was a time in Florida when my third wife, Mil-Jean, told the

Killeen's guys that I didn't want to see or talk to them anymore, which was not true. After a year, Bobby decided to look for me. He was in Florida for something. He found my wife's office at Boca Life magazine. He went to the office and asked for my phone number. The secretary made a call and told Bobby that Mil-Jean was not there. Bobby told her he had time and that he would wait all day if he had to. The secretary made another call. This time, Mil-Jean came out of her office without saying a word, wrote my phone number down for him. That put me in touch with the Killeen's gang again. (That's why I owe him.)

Chapter 19: Another Heartbreak

A Valentines card came back in the mail. Stamped on it were the words, "return to sender." It didn't have enough postage. It was addressed to some guy named Steve in New Jersey. My wife, Miljean, sent it. I had to open it. To my surprise, there were three pages saying, "I love you, I love you, I love you." My heart dropped. Just like my last wife. I guess I just can't hold onto a woman. In anger, I ripped the card in half. Then I stopped and came to my senses putting the card away, thinking why? What did I do wrong? I never cheated on her. It just seems like nothing I do works in a marriage. Just a minute ago I had everything in life I ever wanted. It's just another real-life experience. After a couple of days, I couldn't hold it in any longer. At dinner in a restaurant on the beach in Del Ray, I asked Mil-jean, "how is Steve?" She couldn't speak and walked out of the restaurant. I felt like shit. I still loved her, yet I was mad and didn't know how to handle it. I finished eating and was ready to take a cab home when I saw her sitting in the car. We drove home without saying a word until we arrived at the house.

Then she started telling me how this all went down. It went like this. "She was called by one of her old high school classmates from California who was organizing a class reunion. She would handle the West and Steve, who I never met, would organize the New York, New Jersey area, Mil-jean was to take care of the southern United States. When she called Steve, they would talk on the phone for hours. She said I didn't know him in high school but we found each other in our yearbooks. I finally had to go up to New Jersey and meet him. That's when we got involved with one another."

I felt really bad as she was telling the story. Figure that one out. Here I go again. I got down on my knees and pleaded with her to let me try again. She agreed to try.

Now it came time for the reunion in New Jersey. She said she wasn't going to see him anymore except for the reunion. Off she went. Of course I didn't hear anything from her for four days. Finally she called. The first thing out of my mouth was, did you spend time with him? She couldn't lie and said that she had, but only to find out if she really loved him or not. She said she didn't and that she loved me. I said to myself, "is this going to happen every year?" I told her to see my lawyer when she got back home. I have a way of turning my feelings off. I remember the bad things that she did to me to this day. She doesn't know about the card that was returned in the mail. She thought I had arranged for a private investigator to follow her. The divorce was terrible. She lied, took everything that wasn't nailed down and blamed everything on her lawyer. I wanted to just walk away from the whole thing but my friends, Dick and Milly, wouldn't let me. Milly said: "if you walk away, I'll never talk to you again", and she meant it. They got me to fire my lawyer and brought in their lawyer.

Forced To Live Together

The lawyer told me not to leave the house until it was over. Living with her in a separate room was frustrating. The desire for a sexual encounter overcame the hatred built up between us. One night I swallowed my pride and knocked on her bedroom door. I pleaded with her to give me a sexual hand! Her response was, after a long pause, to come in. (Sex is a strong thing but didn't solve our problems). I never cheated on her, but I learned what it's like to be cheated on. I needed this kick in the ass again!

Mil-jean Trial

The typical settlement trial, lies, lies, lies, lies and lies. It was the worst time of my life. I thought that the trial was for a settlement on what we owned together like boats, cars and homes. I was wrong. It was like a murder trial. My wife's lawyer got me on the stand and handed me some papers and asked me if it were true, that I cheated on my taxes. He also asked if it were true, that I didn't even send Christmas presents to my grandchildren. At that time, the judge intervened and said to my wife's lawyer, "you're a pig!" The lawyer objected. The judge then told the lawyer what a pig is, "a greedy filthy animal." The judge also said, "I don't care what anybody says, he gets half the house." Things aren't so bad after all. I guess I did something right and by the way, I sent my grandchildren checks for Christmas. I walked away from the house. My wife still lives there. What's new? I observed how Mil-Jean's ex-husband had a very difficult time letting her go, but I didn't have any problem after the settlement trial. I couldn't care less what happened to her or who she was with. I just turned her off. Dick and Milly let me use the apartment that they had on the ocean, with a private beach and the Intracoastal right out the front door. It was called Hillsboro Mile. My first morning, I woke up to this bright light coming through the window; it was the sun coming up over the ocean. (It's good to have great friends.)

After The Settlement Trial - Divorce #3 (1992)

It was a Friday night, and I went to a bar called Bennigan's, on Glades Road and the Turnpike, in Boca. I started celebrating this great relief of being embarrassed and rewarded at the same time.

The place was filled with after work people. I decided to buy a round of drinks for the House, which caused a lineup of people telling me about their divorce and settlements and of course buying me a drink. That went on for a couple of hours. I finally decided to go across the street to an upscale bar and restaurant called Pete's, where they had a dance floor and large bar. The waitresses were young and wore skimpy outfits and high heels. The later it got, the more people arrived, and by then I was flying high. I gave this beautiful waitress who had been taking care of me a fifty dollar tip to always make sure that I had a beer in my hand at all times. At the end of the night, the waitress, Nancy, asked me if I wanted to go with her to an all night bar? That's where all the bartenders and waitresses would go after hours. I felt like her father, but what the hell, she was beautiful, and getting better as the night went on. Finally, we ended up in my apartment on the ocean, where I think I had a good time. I do remember her saying that she was going to get married to a guy in the service, and asked me, what did I think about it? I told her about my experiences and I said go for it. If you don't like it you can always bail out. (Thinking to myself, as she's laying in my bed with me that this relationship with this guy couldn't be too strong. She was gone in the morning and all I could think, was "good luck.")

Now I had to retrieve my boat and Hydro Hoist, which was left to me in the settlement. I got John, who worked for me, to help me. John and I had to go to the house and figure out how we were going to get the Hydro Hoist from my dock to  the Banana Boat restaurant location up north. The Hydro Hoist had two pontoons that you pump air into and it lifts the boat, so you can imagine how difficult it is to pull it by boat. John got on the Hydro hoist. We tied some ropes to the boat and started going up the Intracoastal, bumping into docks and other boats. It looked like a wagging tail on a dog. We approached our first bridge. I called to John and asked if we would make it under the bridge? John said, "it looked good," and immediately there was a loud bang. We hit the bridge and had to back off. The bridge tender, opened it up and, long before we arrived at the next bridge that bridge tender opened it, knowing that we were coming. We finally arrived at the Banana Boat Restaurant where I had rented a slip. That's where we had some great times in the future. That same night while I was alone in my apartment the phone rang. To my surprise, it was Karolee, who I hadn't talked to in years. She proceeded to tell me that she was sorry for blaming me for years about everything that went wrong between us. I loved that this was going to open up the relationship between

Karolee and me. It would be good, not only for us, but also for our daughters.

Isn't it interesting that all it took was for someone to swallow their pride and make the effort?

Corvette

One day I was walking by a car showroom and spotted a blue-silver Corvette with a spoiler on it. It was beautiful, and I thought to myself, "why can't I have one?" I went in and asked for the price of the car. They told me and immediately I called Dick and Milly Olson, who handled my money for me. I

told them I needed a cashiers check right away. They didn't ask me any questions, and came as soon as possible to fulfill my dream. They were very happy for me, but thought I paid too much. The salesman said to me that it was the fastest and easiest sale he ever made.   I'm happy.

Pearl

I heard about a dance that was being held at the Holiday Inn in Boca Raton, Florida off of Glades Road and I-95 on Friday nights. Now that I have my new corvette I was off looking for something new. I would go to the bar and sit where I could see the whole floor, trying to catch the eye of someone that appealed to me, like a predator on the prowl. To my surprise, a girl came up to me and asked, "Would you like to dance?" That killed all my wild animal thoughts. She was well dressed, had blonde hair, and a great body. What more could you ask for? Her name was Pearl. It was easy to like her, and we became friends quickly. We would meet on Friday nights and continue our regular lives during the week. No questions asked. We hit all the nightspots that she knew well. Most were in the Palm Beach area. She had one of the greatest wardrobes, at her townhouse. They were two bedrooms; one was filled with racks of clothes, some with the sale tags still on them. She drove a Jaguar and had a house on Long Island, New York, that she rented. Each year, she would enter a look-alike contest. That was held at Pete's restaurant, which I talked about earlier after my settlement trial. Perl entered as Marilyn Monroe, wearing the little white dress and high heels. And of course won the contest. Now you know, what she looked like. After a while, I had the inkling that she was using me to make boyfriends jealous, but in a way. I guess I was using her also. We were intimate and would have great times together, with no strings attached. I guess that's what it's all about. Being a Jewish Princess, and not really knowing anything about domestic things, she threw caution to the wind, buying a pre-cooked chicken and heating it, trying to show me that she could be domesticated. Of course, it was burned almost to the bone. She felt bad, but we both went into a laughing fit, so it was worth the burn. Another time at a bar she grabbed my ass and couldn't get over how hard it was. With a few drinks in her she hollered to the bar, where all the guys were and say, "feel his ass it's so hard". I felt like crawling into a whole. Finally the time came when she had to pull up stakes and go back to New York to straighten out problems with her house. It was great fun! (Love you, Pearl)

Chapter 20: Bad News

We found out that my mother was diagnosed with breast cancer, and immediately had a mastectomy. They said that she was cancer free, but wouldn't you know; after six months, she started having backaches. The next diagnosis was that cancer had moved to her brain. She was put into a hospital in New York State, and quickly went into a coma. I flew up from Florida on American Airlines. I stayed at the hospital for three weeks and decided to return to Florida as my work was piling up. My nephew, Fred, drove me to Newark Airport and I boarded the plane. I had a seat in the rear of the plane. We sat for a long time, when I noticed a stewardess coming down the aisle looking for numbers. When she got to me, she said, 'Mr. Bennett?" There is a phone call for you in the office and we're removing your luggage from the plane now. I knew what that meant. My mother had passed. Fred had been watching the plane and stayed to drive me back to my father's house, that's when I found that I had to pick out the casket for my mother. They had already picked and paid for their plot which made it easier for me, but it was hard. We had the funeral; it was heart breaking for my family and me. During that time, my first wife, Jean, called to give her condolences. After a lot of conversation, she said, "if you stayed with me you could have saved a lot of time and aggravation." She was right. Then we had the best Irish wake party ever at my mother and father's house. We sang my mother's favorite songs. The family members arrived from all over. It was a tremendous party that I will never forget. I returned to Newark Airport and American Airlines a week later. The same group of airline staff was there. They remembered me and changed my seat to First Class. They couldn't do enough for me. People do care. (Thank you American Airlines.)

My Other Daughter, Jessica   1993

Jessica was getting into trouble in New York. Lisa called me in Florida and asked if I would be willing to take her and give her a job? I said that I would, right away. It seems she was with a nightclub crowd, not coming home, plus drugs and who knows what?

Jessica agreed to come to Florida, which was a surprise to Lisa and Karolee. Jessica came right off the bat. One of our first encounters was when Jessica got tough with me when I would tell her what to do. She would give me that face with her right lip raised and eyes squinted, so I gave her the same look right back. This got her to laugh. From then on, we became very close. We would work together, drink together, and on Fridays I would let her use my Corvette to go out on the town. At work I would give her the toughest jobs like spraying a popcorn ceiling with water that would drip down on her face, and then she had to scrape the ceiling off. What a messy job, but she did it. Before work we would have breakfast at her favorite restaurant on the beach, where we could watch the boys playing volleyball in the sand, showing off. Jessica decided to go and spend some time at that beach, I wonder why, so I dropped her off. When she returned with a boy, she explained to me that she walked by the volleyball court, wiggled her fanny, the boys started whistling. She put down her blanket, immediately one of the boys came over to her. His name was Max. He lived in Chicago and was there with a group of his friends. Jessica liked him and brought him home to meet me. He looked me right in the eye and said, "nice to meet you, Mr. Bennett". I could see he was a gentleman and I liked him right away, unlike some of the other boys, who wouldn't even look you in the eye. Max went back to Chicago. They called each other every night, throwing kisses at each other over the phone. She turned to me and said she was going to Chicago. I gave her my blessing. They married, and before you knew it, Jessica was pregnant. I went to Chicago just before the baby was born. When it was time for the delivery, Karolee, Max, and I were there, trying to deliver the baby, while the doctors and nurses watched from cameras. We tried, but were having a hard time. Jessica didn't want drugs. She wanted natural childbirth, but during the delivery she started screaming, "give me drugs"!... so much for natural childbirth. The doctors and nurses came in. Lights came down from the ceiling and they delivered the baby, Max Jr. If I had known that childbirth was that difficult, I probably never would have had any children. I had always been handed the baby in a beautiful wrapped white blanket and I would say, "let's have more." Everything seemed to be fine until the next baby was born. Justin was born with a defective heart and went through all kinds of delicate operations. It took a damaging toll on Jessica.

Justin's Death

I was in Chicago just after one of Justin's operations. He was in the Intensive Care Unit, with many other babies who had similar problems. They were put into incubators with tubes running all over. Some babies were in roller beds, so that they could be moved easily to different locations. Families looked through glass windows with no expression, knowing that they were wishing for some kind of miracle. You felt sorry for them, not thinking of your own problems.

Finally, Justin let go, after 14 months of agonizing pain. At that moment, Jessica picked him up in her arms, not letting anyone take him from her. Even her husband, Max, couldn't retrieve the baby. She held him for hours before she let him go to the nurses. Heartbreaking!

At the burial there was an unfortunate incident. It seems the hole dug for the casket was not large enough. It was very cold, and there were lots of families, young and old. They were holding white balloons that they were going to let go after the burial. Everyone patiently waited. Finally the burial was complete. The balloons were let go. Everyone was looking to heaven. It was very emotional. I got into the car behind the wheel. Jessica sat next to me and Lisa was in the back seat. Jessica put her hand on my knee. I was full of pain for her, and when she touched me, I started crying out of control. I couldn't stop. Jessica held me like I was her baby. That was one of the most difficult feelings that I had ever felt. At times like this, I question if there is a God. At church the next Sunday, the Pastor said, if you blame God for your mishaps that means you believe in him.

Back To Work

I started the day like I always did, with breakfast and an early start on a project. This one was on a wall that we were removing in a condo in Boca. I sent the boys on another job, I was doing this one alone. I had turned off all the breakers, I thought, to the wall and disconnected the wires to the outlets.

I cut the metal conduit and started pulling the wires through. All of a sudden, I couldn't let go of the conduit. I was being electrocuted with 220 volts! It was like my hands were pulsating and glued to it. I pulled on the conduit as hard as I could, I heard circuit breakers go off. I was released and slammed against the front door falling on my face. I laid there for a moment and I had this wonderful relaxed, no pain feeling. It's hard to explain, but I remembered Lee Trevino, a professional golfer, was hit by lightning and said when he woke up in the hospital, "the feeling that he had was hard to explain, but he felt great." Maybe there is something to the shock treatments after all?

Disaster at work

We were working on a large condo project on the beach. It was on the first floor, building a soffit over a 12-inch pipe that ran the full length of the condo. Outside there was a cold front coming through, and the heater for the hallways was located in a room on the roof, 17 stories high. The pilot light that turns the heater on had gone out, so the head maintenance man, Mike, went up to check the problem out. When he tried to light the pilot, the room that he was in turned into an inferno. Gas must have built up from the blown out the pilot light. It was like someone took a flamethrower and turned it on him. Somehow he had the energy to get to the elevator and come down 17 floors. I was working near the elevator on the main floor. When the elevator doors opened, Mike was standing in the elevator with his clothes smoking. I immediately ran into the elevator grabbing him, laying him on the floor, hollering, "get an ambulance, call 911, do something!" I attempted to take his cap off, but couldn't, it was melted to his skull. Finally the ambulance came, it seemed forever, taking him away.

The insurance took care of him, and the people in the condo donated money to him, helping him to a early retirement, the hard way.

The Rotten Kid

There were a few customers of mine who were different. One was the "Rotten Kid". I did some small jobs for him and got into a conversation where he was telling me about all his accomplishments, like his advertising agency trying to buy the Detroit Pistons basketball team and such. As soon as I told him about me taking the Pistons into the Playboy club in Chicago, we suddenly had something in common and became good friends. One time he invited me to dinner at a Palm Beach restaurant to meet his new girlfriend from Detroit. As we were being seated at the table, the Kid said he would be right back. That's when his girlfriend, Wanda, told me that she didn't even know what she was doing there and how pushy the Kid was, he even had a plane, write my name in the sky, saying he loved me, over the Detroit skyline. The Kid returned to the table with a waiter, presenting Wanda with a one-month anniversary cake. That's the last we heard of her. The Kid immediately met someone else, who was very attractive and married her, starting a family right away. He was so proud of his nickname. He even had caps made up in bold print that read "THE ROTTEN KID". He also bought a large boat that was named the same. The Kid asked me if I wanted to go out to sea and shoot at some bottles with his new UZI? I said "no!"

The next thing I heard about was that he ran over a rowboat, putting two people in the hospital. His version was. "What were they doing there anyway!" (That cost him.)

His business was going great. I can see him changing, especially when he was decorating his new penthouse apartment. He would carry a small bag with him filled with cash. When the job was finished he would barter and pay off in cash. It worked!

We would still go out together and work out shooting baskets. Most of the time he would be standing on the foul line passing me the ball for layups, until I finally told him he needed the work more than me, just to get him moving.

The kid was building a mansion in Detroit; he showed me the plans and invited me to come out to see the finished product. I declined as I was trying to distance myself from him. I was just tired of the way he was acting. That was until one day, a real estate woman by the name of Donna, who I was friends with, asked me if I would mention to the Kid that she had just sold a penthouse that had been on the market for over a year. The reason being, she knew the Kid was trying to sell some high-priced real estate that she wanted to get in on. So, reluctantly, I went to his apartment, did a couple of small jobs. While there he showed me a replica of Nathan's hot dog stand in Coney Island that he paid $40,000 for. That's when I casually mention that Donna sold the penthouse that was on the market for years. That led to $1,000.00 cash in my pocket for the tip.

Chapter 21: Agee

The condo where I did most of my work (interior renovations) had over three hundred apartments. This put me in a position to meet numerous single women, one of whom was Agee. I knew her husband before he passed away. He was in the theater ticket business in New York City. I was hanging a lamp for Agee in her kitchenette with John, my friend and employee. I asked Agee how her sex life was. She responded that it was not good. She told us that on her last date, the guy she was with asked her if she was a rich Boca Bitch? (Not good!) After hearing that I suggested that she let me take her out. No strings attached, she agreed to it. I took her to Pete's Restaurant where they had dancing, which I talked about earlier. We had a great time! In our conversation, she told me that she had a house in Long Island, N.Y., a cabin in W. Virginia, and a restaurant off Times Square, N.Y. You know, one of those theater restaurants with a picture of Frank Sinatra on the wall. She said she was going to spend a week at the cabin and invited me join her. I accepted and drove up the next week from Florida.

The log cabin was on top of a mountain. A narrow rough dirt road led the way up to the cabin, which my Corvette couldn't make. Agee had to come down and drive me up in her four-wheeler. It wasn't far from the Greenbrier Country Club. That's where they have the underground bomb shelter for the President and high officials and great golf courses. I stayed overnight in the cabin. In the morning we heard a lot of noise outside. It was a large bear, up in a fruit tree. Agee, I had learned, was an ex marine who they used in the Second World War ads with her picture that read: "JOIN THE MARINES". She had a gun but would never use it unless the bear came into the cabin. Finally the tree fell down and the bear ran off. (It was scary!) When we returned to Florida I would take the whole group out on my boat, a 25' Sea Ray with Rick, his girl, Dawn, John, his girl, and Agee. I would make a run up and down the Intracoastal. When we returned to the dock, at the Banana Boat Restaurant, we drank and ate. They had all kinds of drinks. Some were weird concoctions with names like Sex on the Beach and others. We would drink until we were just about out on our feet. I couldn't drive, so Agee had to drive me home and put me to bed. Of course the next day was not good. (Will I ever learn?) I also visited her home on Long Island and the Times Square restaurant where they made me my favorite meal, Veal Parmesan, but it had a bone in it.

One day one of my other female customers was at the condo pool. She was seated next to Agee, and overheard a woman ask her how she was doing with Richard. Her response was that she didn't have enough money for him. When I was told that, it made me feel like a gigolo. That I am not! I've learned through my Park Avenue days that the last thing I would want was a rich woman to run my life! The only reason that she might have thought that was because I was dating other women in the building and she was saving face. Some of these other women would tell me that they had plenty of money. I guess trying to impress me, but to me their lifestyle just wasn't for me. One woman owned an advertising agency in New York City. She just wanted to travel. That, to me, was dull, and I didn't care if she was the most beautiful woman in the world. It just wouldn't last. I didn't want to give up my lifestyle.

Wilt Chamberlain's Bar

On another occasion I was at Wilt Chamberlains' Bar and Restaurant in Boca Raton, Florida, having a drink with my buddies, John and Rick. A girl joined us. She said she was waiting for her boyfriend and had a few drinks with us. When her boyfriend came in, he had a drink and told us he had to leave for work. Everyone else left, except for the girl and me. I noticed she went to the ladies room a lot, then I suggested that we get something to eat. She agreed. We went to a restaurant down the street and had a nice dinner. Once again, she said she was going to the bathroom. After half an hour, with the restaurant about to

153

close, I decided I was going to look for her. I looked into the stalls in the ladies room. There she was, tied up in her shirt under a toilet bowl, like in a straight jacket, stoned out of her mind. I put her in my car and asked her where she lived? She told me, in a drunken way. I pulled up to the gatehouse. They didn't know her, so I took her to my apartment, a three-story walkup. By now she was passed out and too heavy to move. I had the hardest time getting her back into the car. I thought about going to a first floor motel, but it wouldn't look good, dragging a girl into a motel! I decided to go to my good friend's, Dick and Milly's, who had a long driveway, covered by trees, and sleep it off there. I had to open the windows, as it was hot. That let the mosquitoes in. The gal did wake up a few times and wanted sex. That was definitely out of the question! Finally, the sun came up. She sort of remembered where she lived, thank God. I dropped her off and got out of there! (Another life experience! How the hell did that happen?)

A Great Time

Once again, I met another girl at Wilt Chamberlain's Bar. It was after work and I had a few drinks. She said she was going to a Palm Beach bar at 11 pm, because that's when things start happening. She asked me if I wanted to meet her there. I thought about it and decided I would go, so I went home and took a shower. I got there at 11. The place was mobbed three deep at the bar. They had another bar in the rear, with a large dance floor. I went to the back bar, got a drink and started to walk to the front to look for my date. While passing the dance floor, I couldn't believe my eyes. Two of the most beautiful girls I've ever seen, dirty dancing together with mini skirts and high heels. The guys at the bar were just drooling, watching them. I just couldn't walk by them. I had to join in. I didn't know how they were going to accept me, but it's what a few drinks can do. (They accepted me.) We continued dancing without losing a step, with our heads together like in a huddle introducing ourselves. One of the guys at the bar seeing me cut in, decided he would try to invade our dance party, but was rejected by the girls saying, "we're with Richard". That really made me feel good. I finally asked them to join me for a drink, and that's when they informed me that they were about to start soliciting for a strip club in West Palm Beach that they worked for. But before they started, they told me to meet them Thursday night at 11 p.m. at their club. Then they began handing out their cards. They were fast, knowing what the outcome would be, and were quickly ushered out.

When I turned around, the girl who I was supposed to be meeting there was watching the whole thing. (Oh, well! I had fun anyway!) The meeting at the strip club is another story.

The next meeting at Chamberlain's was a female sergeant in the paratroopers by the name of Bea. She had 85 jumps and looked like she could be a sergeant if you know what that means. As we drank she started to tell me stories, the last one was tragic. She was making her last jump and everything was going as expected until one of the shoots of the paratrooper behind her didn't open. He grabbed onto her as he was falling.

Here they were, face to face, with both shoots now getting entangled, falling to earth screaming in fear, hitting the ground, luckily in a muddy area, if you can say that. The other trooper went into a coma for three months. Bee had broken ribs and a fractured back, but through all this, when the other trooper came out of his coma, he had lost his two legs and went back to jumping again. How about that? She managed a steakhouse and invited me to come there. I went and met all the waitresses. Afterwards we went up to her apartment. We made out for a while and finally had sex. Bee acted funny, she started crying, and went into her bedroom and closed the door. I sat there not knowing what to do, listening to her cry until she finally fell asleep. This situation is uncommon. What most males are looking for, when they meet someone new is the anticipation and excitement. Boy this was different, I snuck out and that was that.

Again, at Wilt Chamberlain's, I was with John when we met a girl whom John ended up marrying. It didn't last. After a few years, they went through a divorce. John suffered from depression and the whole scene was so very difficult on him. He ended up taking his own life.

John never really told us what his problem was. My first reaction to his taking his own life was that I was pissed off. Then reality set in. Then sorrow. John's parents were the greatest! A perfect mother and father! They completely spoiled him, and they loved him deeply and would have done anything for him.

John's funeral was in New Jersey. Rick and I were pallbearers. We still talk about John a lot. He is kept alive in our memories. We still keep in touch with his family. (Life can be tough.)

Chapter 22: Lisa and Me

While in New York, Lisa often tried to fix me up with some of the neatest women. I met one for dinner at a little restaurant on West 23rd Street. Lisa was with her latest boyfriend, Dr. Bob Giller. When I arrived, they were all there. My date was beautiful, with a body that wouldn't quit! Her name was Gloria. We had a nice dinner. When leaving, we shared a cab with Lisa and Dr. Giller. They dropped us off at Gloria's apartment on 59th and 5th Avenue, overlooking Central Park and the Plaza Hotel, probably the highest priced real estate in New York City.

Gloria was great and made me feel very comfortable. We had a couple of drinks. We then made a date to meet in Florida. Later, Lisa told  me Gloria was the mistress of one of the richest real estate men in New York City. (Oh boy!) Gloria and I did meet in Florida. I picked her up and we went to a local restaurant and talked about anything and everything. Things were going well until I said the wrong thing. It was when I told her this was helping me to forget all about my ex-wife. She hit the roof! She wanted to know if I was using her? I responded that I didn't even really know you. The whole exchange pissed her off. I suggested that we leave the place and took her home. I guess the reason why she got so mad was that others were always using her, being a mistress on call. I saw her again at Lisa's engagement party, on Park Avenue and 71st Street at Nancy's (Dr. Giller's business advisor) apartment. Karolee was there with the boyfriend who had moved into my house right after I left. I tried not to look at him. Then Gloria walked in with short white hair, a white tight mini skirt and legs that wouldn't quit. She was stunning. I just can't believe what a few wrong words can do to a relationship. She glanced at me and turned away. (That's that.)

Lisa's Fiancé

Dr. Bob Giller, a well-established physician, had an office and town house on Park Avenue and a large mansion in the Hamptons. Pretty nice! I loved it when I arrived at LaGuardia Airport from Florida, a limo was waiting for me to take me to the townhouse on Park Avenue. Dr. Giller was about 20 years older than Lisa, but she said she loved him. That was good enough for me, in the old days. He ran with Andy Warhol's crowd. How about that? They finally got engaged. It was going to be a big affair. People would be coming in from Europe, and all over the states. I was at the mansion with Bob Giller, Lisa, and his advisor, Nancy, sitting in the living room. Nancy said to Lisa that she was now going to be a part of a higher class of society. I cringed. Lisa glanced over at me. I wondered what was going through her mind, I bet that she was wondering the same about me. Later when we were alone, she said that she almost died knowing how I felt about the whole class thing. Giller also told Lisa that her career in modeling and yoga wasn't enough, so he had her start law school at Hunter College in New York City, to which she agreed. I don't think it was whole hearted though.

Nancy, Dr. Giller's advisor (whatever that means), lived on 71st Street and Park Avenue. She was an attractive woman. She offered to let me stay in her apartment for a couple of nights before I returned to Florida. I accepted. The first night, she showed me to my room. It was a big place. I suggested that we could share her bed and watch a movie together. She agreed to it. It was great. The only trouble was that Dr. Giller found out about it and didn't care for it at all, he naturally complained to Lisa. Tough!

We also went to a Park Avenue style party at Giller's townhouse.   The waiters and waitresses wore tuxedos and we wore sweaters and jeans. It was winter, and we were very comfortable. The people who were there were professional people, one was a movie director and his wife who had just one an Oscar. His wife kept saying to me that she knew me from somewhere. Maybe she read Playboy? We sat on the floor, told and listened to stories about Hollywood, murder trials and such. When it came to my turn, I talked about Playboy, which drew a lot of attention. Lisa fit right into this crowd, beautiful and outstanding. I was so proud of her, not knowing at this time, if the world she's in is really screwed up or not! I was treated like someone and that made me feel good. I had no problem talking to people, once I was confident. It was fun.

Then Lisa was presented with the pre-nuptial papers. It was like Giller was purchasing something on time. He agreed to give Lisa a large amount the first year of their marriage, doubling it the next and so on. When she told Giller that the way it was written, it made it look like he was buying her. She finally walked out on him. Everything for the wedding was paid for, including the money her mother and I had put up. Dr. Giller had contributed substantially more. Lisa gave back everything of value he had given her. Giller tried to reconcile with her but to no avail. That's my girl. That's the best way to learn about life. She's catching up to me.

5th Avenue

Lisa introduced me to another woman, Jan, who lived on Fifth Avenue in the upper 70s. We had a dinner date where she told me that she was engaged to a polo player from

South America, who Prince Charles of England loved to play polo with. She invited me to stay in her apartment that night. Nice! In the morning she asked what I might like for breakfast. I responded bacon and eggs would be good. I thought she was going to make it. Instead, she picked up the phone and ordered it from a restaurant on Madison Avenue. She also let me use one of her cars to visit Gina and my two aunts on Long Island. I took the Mercedes to make me look good. Jan had a townhouse at the Wellington Polo Club in Florida. This was just off the polo field, where Prince Charles, Diana, and Jan's fiancé could just walk onto the field. After they left I went to the apartment where Jan showed me pictures of her fiancé and the Queen Mother. She was proud of that. She decided to do over the apartment and replace rugs, which were like new. She gave me the old ones, so John and I put them in my apartment on Hillsboro mile. Jan reminded me that Prince Charles and Princess Diana had stepped on these rugs. I told her that I would put flags where they stepped. Jan also asked me to go with her to a polo awards night in Wellington, Florida. I sort of hesitated but, what the hell. I'll see what this world is all about. The first award was to a young girl on the podium, hosted by William DeVane. I will never forget what she said, and how she said it. "I want to thank my father and mother for the string of polo ponies that they gave me." Here I am, a kid from Brooklyn, listening to this crap. It seems money is no object. Jan also gave me a key to the Wellington apartment in case I needed it. You never know....

Back In New York

Jan decided that a group of us were going to do something good for the underprivileged. On Thanksgiving day, there was a church in downtown Manhattan that she set up with turkey dinners. Each of us was to take one table of 10

160

vagrants and serve them as much as they wanted. Prior to the event we all met at Jan's apartment on 5th Ave. We arrived in jeans and casual shirts; Jan came out dressed to the nines. We asked why she was dressed like that? She responded, "How are they going to know who has the money (wow)!" After we served them, we sat and listened to some of their stories. There were some interesting stories about losing jobs and families along with others about drugs and drinking. Most of them were set in their ways. I doubted they would ever get back to reality. (They took the wrong road.)

Another Time With Jan

Jan and I had made a date to go out for New Years, since her fiancé was always out of the country anyway. Jan's sister asked if she could join us with her husband and 10-year-old son. Jane didn't get along with her sister, because when their parents passed away, they couldn't agree on what to sell, like the Rolls-Royce that Jan wanted to get rid of, little things like that. Jan asked me to arrange the evening, what the heck do I know about that. I suggested dinner at the Howard Johnson's hotel where her sister was staying; and going bowling, which was nearby, figuring it would be fun for the boy. Not knowing that he wasn't well. He was rather quiet and didn't say much, just nodded his head in response to questions. But he came alive when he started bowling and even smiled when he knocked some pins down. It was fun, but the next day he had a relapse. Poor kid. But he DID have fun.

Meeting At Gino's

Gino's Restaurant was my favorite place to eat in New York City. It was Italian of course, and cash only. It was located on Lexington Avenue and 61st. When I would fly into LaGuardia airport, I would meet Lisa there. The place was

161

always crowded so we had to wait at the bar most of the time until a table was available. This one time while at the bar, we met a woman who was waiting for her girlfriend. She was an agent, her name was Barbara and she loved Lisa's look. We asked her to join us. Her friend arrived so the four of us sat down and talked. Barbara had offices in New York and California. She had all kinds of top people with her agency including all of the astronauts. Her girlfriend created handmade sweaters, costing $1,500 and up, (not bad!) I was headed to New Jersey to be with my father for a couple of days, as we were getting ready to leave, Barbara asked me if I wanted to go to the Broadway show, "Gypsy", starring Tyne Daley? It was for the next evening. I thought for a minute. It meant that I would have to come back to the city, which I didn't care for, however, she wasn't bad looking, so I agreed to the date. She told me to meet her at Toots Shores. I was right on time the next evening. We had a drink and saw the show. Our seats were terrific, overhanging the right side of the stage. It was like a private show. Afterwards, we went back to Toots Shores, into the restaurant section. They gave us menus, but she demanded the celebrity menus. They exchanged the menus for the celebrity menus, which gave a 50% discount. Maybe they thought I was a celebrity. Ha! We had a nice dinner and then went up to her apartment. She showed me all kinds of celebrity pictures taken with her. I tried to make a move on her, but it didn't work. She was strictly interested in Lisa and some modeling jobs that she thought would be good for her. I left well enough alone. We left on good terms. Right Place Right Time again!

Modeling

The following week I went on a job with Lisa, not knowing it was for lingerie. Luckily it was with a female

162

photographer and art director. Lisa really knew how to move. She was a photographer's delight that translates into getting more shots in the hour. Lingerie models get time and a half and double-time. Lisa gave them every dollar's worth. That's why they keep hiring her. (I was proud of her.)

Religion

Another Lisa time was when she called me from Bosnia; a country she wanted to see because that's where someone sighted an Angel years ago. She was always looking for the right religion. She finally found peace with yoga. While we were talking on the phone, I asked what the noise was in the background? She told me it was bombing, but not to worry. They don't bomb where I am! I told her to get out of there, now! (Kids!)

Another Time

Just before Lisa left for Europe, she bought a new Trans Am car saying that: "if anyone ever bothered me, I could get away fast". She put the car away and told her boyfriend at that time, Eddie, not to touch it while she was gone. Of course, as soon as Lisa left, he took the car to a nightclub. When he came out, the car was gone. Eddie was now in big trouble. The police were notified and recovered the car within a couple of days. The car was held in the police compound. When Lisa came back from Europe and went to pick up the car at the compound, it wasn't there. It was stolen from the police department, and never found again. Go figure.

Lou Savarese

Lisa knew that I liked the sport of boxing. She said she had a surprise for me. She told me to go to Madison Square Garden, front entrance. There would be a heavyweight boxer, undefeated at that time, and his name was Louis Savarese. He was a good friend of Lisa's. I met him. We went into the arena and watched the fights. In between fights, all the boxers and promoters would come up to him and he would introduce them to me. I guess they thought I was a promoter. After the fights we went across the street to a bar where we met three of his

buddies and a new promoter looking to back Lou. We had a drink and Lou was on his best behavior. When it came time to leave, we said goodbye to the new promoter. As he walked away, Lou grabbed my arm and said, do I have to break your arm to go have a few more drinks? I said, "let's go". The first bar we went to was close by, filled with well dressed men and woman.

I noticed two attractive women at the bar that a couple of guys were working on; probably buying them drinks for a while. With a couple of drinks in me, I really had no problem cutting into their action, then inviting Lou and his entourage

164

over. We talked and joked with them for a while, getting phone numbers and the usual things and had no problems, from the two poor guys. (I was bad.) We went to another bar, located in the upper West side, by the name of Blondie's. Of course two blonde girls ran it. I was drinking and talking to the blondes. A good-looking guy came in and started cutting into my conversation. We had words. Then Lou came over and the guy backed off. I just had to introduce Lou, just to bust his chops. "This is Lou Savarese, 35 and 0, heavyweight boxer." The other guy gulped. It's nice to have backup. Blondie told the guy that I was from Florida. All of a sudden he was my best friend because he said he was moving to Florida to open a bar. He gave me his card. And that was that! Lou drove me back to Tudor City where Lisa was staying. She waited up for me to find out what happened. I told her I had the time of my life and collapsed into bed. Lou called Lisa the next day and said "boy, your father's very aggressive", whatever that means. Lou is such a good guy. When Lisa wanted to go rollerblading at 2 a.m. in the morning, she would call Lou and off they would go down to Wall Street and back uptown again. I guess he was a bodyguard. Then Lisa met a new boyfriend by the name of Charles Matkin. Charles was a yoga teacher and matched Lisa well. They were married in the real Woodstock. They fit right in to the area. A yoga guru married them. They started teaching yoga together in their new home in Garrison, New York, and a studio in New York City. They even taught me yoga, on how to meditate and breathe properly, which helped me mentally and physically. It makes life much more acceptable and worth living. As you get older, I recommend it highly.

Boat Trip

There was a time when Lisa and Charles went on a boat trip to the islands, invited by a young millionaire who was interested in backing them in a new yoga studio. I was to pick them up when they returned. I asked my new girlfriend, Pat, to join us. When they arrived they had to go through customs, which took a long time because Charles was a Canadian and had the wrong papers. While we were waiting in the Miami port, Lisa told us that on the trip there were only 12 people. Each person had their own attendant to give them anything that they needed or wanted. The weather was perfect. The people were great and the food was exquisite. Charles' paperwork was straightened out. We left and went to a local restaurant. There were six of us seated at the table, Lisa, Charles, Pat, me, and two friends from the trip. We were all having a good time. There was a large group at another table that seemed to be drinking heavily. One of the girls from the other table came over and was slightly inebriated. She started talking to Lisa, telling her how beautiful she was and how lucky she was to have Charles. Then she started going around the table, making comments about each person. When she got to me, she said, "and you're okay" and she went on to the next person. At that point, we all decided it was time to leave and so did the other group. We were all out in the parking lot, when the girl came up to me and asked, "could I hold you?" Catching me off guard while the group in the background was calling her. She asked, "can I kiss you?" She did. Pat was having a fit, Lisa and Charles were having a big laugh watching the whole scene. I did grab the girl on the hips with my two hands and pushed her away. I quickly got into the car, knowing that Pat was pissed. I was in a no win situation, and of course Pat wouldn't talk to me for days. (Women.)

Phoenix Rehab 2003

My daughter, Lisa, had an eating disorder, like most models. This, along with a drinking problem made her decide to put herself into a rehab center in Phoenix, Arizona for a month. The people who ran the center wanted the family to join her for a week to see how things were run. There were hundreds of men and women there. It was like being in school that was run by psychiatrists. Before most classes we had to read a confidential pledge in front of family and patients, that was hard for me but I did it. The facility had us go to different classrooms. It was all day classes with the same families. It was like they wanted everyone to listen to all the other patients' problems. Nearing the end of the week, they had Lisa sit in front of me, facing me with all the families around us. She had to tell me what she liked and disliked about me in front of the other families. She told me that she loved me so much that she always compared her boyfriends to me. That made it very difficult for her. I was asked what I thought about that. I responded that I really didn't care what she said, because I loved her and "that's that!" She also told a story about the one and only time I hit her. She was about ten years old. It went like this. Lisa told me that she had cleaned her room. I told her that if she hadn't, I would spank her. I went up to the room and found she had put everything under the bed. I had to stand up to my word and reminded her of the intended spanking. She began to cry hysterically, so I put her over my knee and gave her a tap. Because of the hysteria, the story that she told them was that I hit her with a belt. This is a daughter who I had never hit before. (Things get bigger in the minds of the youth.) When we would eat with Lisa in a large cafeteria filled to capacity with people, Lisa would have to take her plate up to a desk to be checked for what she had eaten. The patients were watched very closely. It worked, according to Lisa. She believed it was very successful, and returned to New York very happy.

Chapter 23: A Love Affair With NO Sex

I was hired by a decorator for a job in an apartment overlooking the Atlantic Ocean located in Boca Raton, Florida. Our job was to put a signature kitchen ceiling in. The place was a mess; priceless paintings and clothing were all over the place. It was hard to work because of all the stuff everywhere getting in the way. One of these was a grand piano, with the legs cut off. It was being prepared so a glass top could be put on it. The top had to be in two pieces and lifted up by a crane, because it was too large to fit in the elevator. This was to be used to make a dining room table that would seat 12. A Rodin on a precarious stand in the corner made things even worse. One day while we were working, the owner, Diane, came in. She was very attractive, but very businesslike. She said, "hello, Mr. Bennett", picked up a few things and left when the project was near ending. There seemed to be a problem with billing, so the decorator kept the legs of the piano. I didn't want to get between them and their lawsuits, so I stayed out of it as long as I got paid. Diane never got the legs, but I'm sure she took that out in other ways. About a month later, I walked into Capital Lighting to pick up some fixtures for a job I was doing, when I noticed Diane. I went over to her, and we talked. She told me that she had just bought another apartment in that same building for her mother and father and wanted me to look at it. The chance meeting started a long relationship with Diane. Allow me to share it with you.

Diane belonged to the Boca Raton Hotel and Club. She played golf there, and often invited me to play. Everything was going well with us, so I decided to make reservations for the two of us for a two-day golf package in Orlando at the Hyatt Hotel. It was the honeymoon package with a free bottle of champagne. The whole works. The first night, I thought that I was going to get lucky as we crawled into bed. I turned to her; she backed away and said that if we had sex, it would ruin our relationship. I thought, well okay, I didn't want to rock the boat. She definitely had a complex about men using her. I pursued the problem, so she began telling me a story about when she took over her oil company that was part of a multi-million-dollar divorce settlement. At her first board meeting, with all men, she was prepared to go into the meeting not to be run over and do it in a nice way. She took a deep breath, walked in and told the board, "lets get this straight. I'm running this blank place, and if you don't like it, get out now!" That was smooth and to the point, but that was Diane. Diane and her business friends always made me feel uncomfortable. At least that's the feeling I had when I was around them. Maybe they thought I was trying to take advantage of her? One time we were at an event and one of her wealthy business friends came up to us. We were standing with drinks in our hands. He cut between us with his back to me and started a conversation with Diane. That really pissed me off, so I walked away, looking for a conversation with anyone who would talk to me. Finally Diane retrieved me, seeing I was mad. I guess she wanted to appease me.

She asked me if I wanted to go to Houston for her daughters wedding? I said, "Yes, this sounds like fun". I also thought I could see what her world was like. When I arrived in Houston, a gay guy picked me up at the airport, who I think didn't care for me. When I said Di, rather than Diane, he corrected me, like my mother would. We arrived at a large home, the gay guy left me and ran off. I think he was jealous that Diane was interested in me. Oh well! I didn't know who lived there, or anyone except Diane. When I walked into the living room filled with people, a woman in a tight red dress came up to me and with a strong Texan accent said, "howdy, my name is Reva, you must be Richie? Diane told me you were coming." Then Reva began telling me about all the companies that she had, I was very impressed. She showed me around, introducing me to everyone saying how everything in Texas was done in a big way. She then introduced me to this other woman by the name of Ann. We hit it off right away. She was from LA and asked me to go to another party with her. Diane wasn't around, so I agreed to go. She had wheels, so there was no problem in getting back to the hotel where arrangements were made for me. We arrived at the party in a high-rise overlooking Houston. It was a crowded room. We were sitting near the front door when it opened. There were two young boys, about 15 or 16 years of age, giggling and nervous. The hostess ran to the door, spoke briefly and closed the door. I asked Anna what that was all about. It seems that she gives them pot for sex. I didn't like the situation so I suggested we leave. It was a weird crowd. I thought that Ann might be like that also, so I had her drop me off at the hotel. She told me I would see her the next day at the wedding. I was still unsure about her. The reception was held at the Museum of Art. (Nice to have connections.) They had me sitting on the balcony with a great group of eight people, looking down on most of the other tables. Down below was Ann, looking up at me, waving her hand to come down and sit with her, but I couldn't believe this one beautiful blonde sitting next to me, who ended up in my room that night. I didn't get to spend any time with Diane. I briefly met Diane's sister, Nicki, not knowing that we would have a long, ongoing affair, later on. (Back to Boca.)

Nicki

I was to meet Diane at her apartment in Boca. I arrived on time, but Diane was late, her sister, Nicki, was there having come in from Huston. We talked for a while, then Nicki said let's get out of here, grabbing her bag we headed down the elevator. Arriving at the ground floor, the door opened, and Diane was standing there. Nicki told Diane that we were going to meet a friend of hers from Tampa, Diane stood there with her mouth open. We then ran off while Nicki was laughing and ended up in my apartment, which was the one on the beach. We started drinking wine and ended up on the beach that night with a full moon, naked as jaybirds. I can still hear her on top of me saying something complicated like flip me up, being slightly intoxicated I did. She disappeared over my head for a long time. I didn't move, when she walked around from behind me, and in her little voice told me that I almost broke her neck. Until this day, I don't know what she was thinking. I asked her later, she didn't know either. Don't try this at home.

Nicki invited me to her place in Tampa, Florida for the weekend. It was one of the most fun filled times. I would make that trip every chance I could get. Her ex-husband was an ex-pro golfer who had a temper. He was abusive. That's why she divorced him. He would call, drunk. I heard a couple of calls. What a jerk! Nicki had her own little business selling jewelry to stores. One weekend, she had a spot in a bridal convention to sell her jewelry. She asked me if I wanted to go? I said yes, it sounded like fun. We arrived in her Dodge convertible with the top down, so we could get all the stuff in. Thank God it didn't rain. The trip was a good 45 minutes. We set everything up. The people started coming in, naturally, all

171

mothers and daughters. That's when Nicki remembered she forgot some of the very important jewelry. She told me to take care of everything; the prices were on the jewelry. She left to go back to her apartment. I hated this. I figured I had nothing to lose, so I started acting like a carnival salesman. It was embarrassing, but I said step right up and get the finest jewelry that money could buy. It worked! The place was filled with young brides and mothers. I was wheeling and dealing, Nicki finally came in, it was just about closing time. She had a great sense of humor and started laughing. That's what I loved about her.

Nicki also would arrange for me to play golf with some men in her country club. She said, they are real good guys, one of them was an electrician and repaired my dildo. (A dildo is a female satisfaction, instrument.) This one was computerized, made in China, it would go in and out, around, up and down with the push of a button - what the hell does she need me for? Now I knew why the guys were snickering?

Nicki worked out, most every other day. She asked me to go with her. I said okay. She proceeded to tell me that she lifted this much weight. Since you are a man, you'll use heavier weights, more push-ups, more sit-ups and leg weights. I finally quit after a couple of hours. We were walking by the basketball court. I said to Nicki, let me show you how I shoot baskets. I was going to put on a show for her. I picked up the ball and was going to shoot. That's when I realized I couldn't raise my arms. I couldn't even raise a fork to my mouth for two days. She got the biggest laugh out of that and I felt like a jerk. These fun days couldn't last, because Nicki received an offer to move to Dallas and work for a company there. She made the decision to go. The weekend Nicki was to leave, Diane and I stayed with Nicki, just the three of us. We watched the Rocky Horror Picture Show (a cult movie) in bed together. What a way to go. Now I am left with Diane. After Nicki moved I called a few times and then we lost contact. (But we had a ball.)

Diane

Diane was Fortune 500 until the government put a cap on the wells. The oil in Houston was going downhill. She wanted to diversify. She began to buy real estate. I was invited to a bank foreclosure in Boca Raton with Diane and Reva from Houston (the woman in red). She was just as tough as Diane. That's why Diane liked her. One had to put up $15,000 to get into the bidding. The first apartment to go on the block was a penthouse. The bidding was opened. No one responded. They had to start somewhere, so Reva called over one of the runners. She slipped him a note with an opening bid of $350,000 for the penthouse with a service elevator, a passenger elevator, and an entrance like a basketball court. The auctioneer on the podium was so happy to get started. He announced the opening bid of $350,000. He waited for a response, but no one responded. It seemed they were waiting to steal some of the smaller apartments, so the bid held and of course a fortune was later made on the sale of it. (Not bad.)

Diane asked me to go to Hot Springs, Arkansas, with her to meet all of her high society friends and parents. We played golf and partied. At one of the parties, I met a woman named Jodi, who was recently divorced from one of the top racehorse trainers. We ended up together in her house for two days with the heavy-duty drapes closed. You didn't know if it was day or night. All of a sudden the phone rang, breaking the silence. The call was to inform her that President Clinton was coming into town. She told me she had to go. I asked her what the call was about; she said I'm a good friend of the family. I'll be back in four hours, I asked her to bring me back something. So I kept myself busy fishing. After a half day, she returned and gave me a picture of her standing next to the

president's limousine. I always wondered if he was getting a piece of that with his reputation. I finally returned to Diane's apartment. She was angry. She said she had brought me here and I disappeared for three days. I always remembered what she said. (We're just good friends.)

I started going around with Diane, meeting her friends. Most of them were on the lake with trams to take you up and down to the water because of the steep hills. One of the ladies who I met with Susan told me to make sure I was using condoms with Jodi. How did she know about that? I guess Diane knew where I had been for the last few days. We looked at some property Diane owned, about a thousand acres overlooking the big lake. We talked about turning it into a golf course with a signature par three hole shooting down to an island green. (Sounds great.) The one thing that I couldn't get over was all of the jade stones. They were all over the property on top of the ground. They were beautiful and selling in stores for big bucks. That night we had a gathering at Diane's house, which had two floors overlooking the lake. They were fun drinking times. We would go into laughing fits until you almost got sick. In the middle of all this, a call came in from a real estate agent. Someone wanted to rent Diane's house, but wasn't interested. The agent replied: "Do you know who the people are? She said: "No." The agent replied: "It's the actors Antonio Banderas, Melanie Griffith and her family." Diane's response was, "do you know who I am?" and hung up. That's my girl! The next day I decided it was time to get back home. Diane asked me if I would drive her new car that she had just bought back to Florida. I told her I would, it was a Mercedes 500 convertible, Black, (oh boy). On the way back to Florida, I was unfamiliar with the buttons and pressed the wrong one that made the seat hot. It mixed with the a/c and steam filled the car. I thought it was going to blow up until I realized what the problem was. I stopped at New Orleans during the day. It looked like crap, but at night, it was lit up like a Christmas tree. I decided to head home. I didn't want to take a chance with Diane's car. I was supposed to stop in Dallas to see Nicki, but decided it was just too far, so I blew her off. That was bad. On the way back I couldn't help singing that song, "I had the time of my life".

Houston Oil

After arriving safely back in Florida with no dents, Diane called and asked me to attend a fund raising dinner-dance and auction in Houston that she couldn't attend. It was mainly given for oil people. My date was Reva. She was named Businesswoman of the Year" for two years in a row. I packed my tux, flew into Houston, was picked up by a limo and was taken to Reva's house. I felt like a big shot. At the function Reva and I danced and drank. She told me that Marty wanted to dance with me. This gal happened to own the Denver Nuggets Basketball team at one time and had settled for 100 million at the time of her divorce. She was a doll! The only problem was that she had a jealous boyfriend with her. (Oh what the hell! She is worth it. She was tall, blond, and well

175

built!) As we were walking to the dance floor, the boyfriend started hollering at her. She hollered back. I figured that I was really into it now, but Marty came to me and we began dancing while the boyfriend just watched. I think that I was used to bust the boyfriends' balls! Then the auction started. The first thing that they started bidding on was a mink stole and Reva started the bidding with $5,000, finally getting it for $15,000. It was exciting. Afterward, we went to another bar where all the oil characters hang out-backslapping, wildcatters, the John Wayne type! They thought I was an oil baron, so I acted the part. Reva loved it!

We finally left the wild gathering and went back to Reva's place. We got comfortable and turned on some music. Reva came in wearing a skimpy little nighty. She pulled out all her minks from the closet and threw them on the floor. We jumped on them. I was horny! When I made my move, she told me it wouldn't be a good idea. Diane wouldn't like it. After all, Diane was the money behind the business and Reva was under the impression that I belonged to Diane, so I backed off. It was very hard. That's funny! When I went to bed with Diane, she said that if we had sex, it would ruin our friendship. Now I want to go to bed with Reva, but she's afraid of Diane. What the hell is going on! At least I got to meet and date all of the women that Diane introduced me to.

The next morning, Diane arrived from Dallas, unexpectedly. Reva and I both knew that nothing happened between us, but we got the feeling that Diane didn't believe us. That evening, we all went out to dinner. Everything was going fine, until Diane told me that she was ready to buy some apartments. She suggested that I could work on them and we could split the profits 50-50. Reva then got involved, saying that she could raise the money and be involved. Diane got very angry and started yelling at Reva, making her cry. I asked Diane what in the hell was she doing? She responded, "I just wanted to show her who was the boss!" (I think she thought that Reva and I had done something together.)

The next morning I was leaving early on a flight back to Florida and Marty came over to say good-bye. What a send off! Three beautiful women, and I didn't even get lucky.

Chapter 24: Prison

One night back in Boca, a Saturday, about 2a.m., while I was sleeping, the phone rang. It was Reva from Houston, Texas. She told me that Diane had just been arrested and would I go to the Palmetto Entrance to the Boca Hotel, where the arrest happened. I was to see if the Mercedes was there and check on Diane at the Boca Jail. The car, as it turned out, had been towed to the jail in Boca. I entered the jail and was told that Diane was being taken to the West Palm Beach jail. I said that I would follow her down there. I was told that I couldn't, but I should go to the West Palm Beach jail and wait for her to arrive. This was about 4 a.m. At around 6 a.m. a lawyer came in to see Diane. They wouldn't allow me to see her, just lawyers were allowed. I kept in touch with Houston, letting them know what was happening. It was Sunday morning. I couldn't get over how many people came in to see their boyfriends, fathers, or family members in jail. They came all dressed up like they were going to church! It was sad to see the children and mothers. What kind of a life do they have to look forward to? Finally, Diane came out, totally exhausted, she showed her anger. She thanked me for being there even through her anger.

The story on how it all happened went something like this. While Diane was driving home, someone hit her car with a stone. She saw two boys, stopped the car, and started hollering at them. They started hollering back. Diane called the police. The officer who came was a woman. Diane was excited and started hollering again. Things got out of hand. The officer, frustrated, called her a Boca Bitch! Diane lost it. Then the officer arrested her. When it ended up in court, the judge asked the officer if she knew that the boy who threw the rock was the mayor's son? She responded, "yes!" The case was thrown out!

Another Time

I was at the Boca Raton Hotel Tower Restaurant with Diane, Reva and a visiting countess. There were two young girls making a commotion at the adjoining table. They were a little intoxicated. Reva decided she had had enough! She told the girls to keep it down. They told Reva to shut up! It was just like some guys fighting with words. I just stayed out of this one. I guess they noticed Reva's accent. It turned out they were all from Texas. The girls asked if she knew who they were and gave Reva their names. Reva proudly said, "no but my name is Reva Stetson." The two girls backed off. I guess Reva won the fight of names. That's the way the Texas Blue Bloods fight it out! The countess wasn't impressed, nor was I. The next day I was on the putting green at the Boca Raton Hotel Golf Club, waiting for Diane. It was quiet and calming, when all of a sudden, the clatter of golf shoe spikes hitting the cement path was heard on the way to the pro shop. It was Diane. Someone had just run into the rear of her Ferrari. It was a big old Lincoln that hit her, an older lady who immediately called her husband. He said he would have a friend of his fix it. He had no clue that everything on a Ferrari has to be replaced and registered. It's rather funny as just the past week; Diane and I were a bit bombed and were trying to blow the engine in the Ferrari because she didn't like it. We couldn't do it! She also hated it when I would grind the gears, me too. Now we had to play golf with a couple of Diane's friends. The gentleman told me, he thought we should give strokes. I asked, "What do you want?" He said two strokes, and I agreed, but Diane didn't like that at all. We played and lost. We went back to the clubhouse for a drink. I could see Diane was extremely mad and wouldn't talk to me, I finally decided that I better leave. I went to kiss her on the cheek; she turned away, which made me a little angry. I took off for New York for a couple weeks to visit my father and sisters. When I returned to Florida, I had a message on my answering machine from Diane saying that she forgave me for being so stupid. That was her way of apologizing to me. I went back to her exciting world.

She had all the girls come into town for a party in the Great Hall at the Boca Raton Hotel. They came from Dallas and Houston, Texas, Aspen, Colorado, and Little Rock, Arkansas. Diane wanted to find new faces for escorts. I asked her how she would do that? She said to go look for them at bars, nightclubs and restaurants. Well, we did. We had fun watching Diane at work. We ended up with a dentist, a manager of a drugstore and Rick and John. It was like going fishing for people.

We all met at Diane's' apartment for a few drinks, dressed to kill, with a few get acquainted tongue kisses, and then we were on our way to the Ball. Pulling up to the Grand Hotel in two limousines, it was almost anticlimactic, compared to the preparation. The Ball was like being at the royal inauguration. When we returned to Diane's place, there wasn't enough room for all the girls. As a consequence, Nancy went home with me to my apartment for two days. She was then going to leave for a week of golf school in south Florida. The next morning, I went to work and Nancy stayed on the beach soaking up the sun. It was fun.

Donald Trump

Another introduction by Diane to me was Jackie, her grandfather owned the Dallas Cowboys. Dandy Don Meredith baby-sat her when she was a little girl. That should have been fun; Jackie was staying with Richard King of King World, who lived on Hillsboro Mile on the beach in Florida. This was just down the street from Dick and Milly's apartment where I lived.

Jackie and I were going to dinner one night with Richard King and his wife. We decided that we would first stop at Mar-a-Lago to see Donald Trump at one of his parties. Richard said he would meet us at the restaurant after. We walked into the main living room at Mar-a-Lago, which was very crowded, Donald saw Jackie come in. He ran over to us and acknowledged Jackie. She introduced me and he then told me that she (Jackie) was lots of fun. Indeed, she was! He asked where Richard King was? The reason that Richard didn't come in was that Trump would be after him for money, to invest in something or other. King didn't want to be annoyed. After a drink and people watching we left for the restaurant to meet up with Richard King and his wife. There were other friends of King there. As we drank and ate through dinner I started to feel uncomfortable as conversations were going by me like I wasn't even there. I started to think... what in the hell am I doing here? But it was just another experience.

The next night Diane, her friend from Wall Street and me were invited to dinner at Jackie's relative's house, where she was staying that night. I was to be Jackie's date. I drove up with Diane and the gentleman from Wall Street. Nice guy!

He didn't take any of her shit! It was a large dinner party. I was at the main table with Jackie. Diane and her boyfriend were seated in the garden. I could see them and gave her the look, as if to say, "I'm sitting at the main table and you're not!" Ha, ha! That killed her! The night was ending; Jackie's girlfriend was trying to talk me into staying over. I had already made arrangements for a golf game in the morning. Diane was behind me, telling me not to stay. I finally said, "no!" The girlfriend said, "your room is right next to Jackie's" with a wink. I said, "no!" She came back with, "Are you too cheap to take a cab in the morning?" That did it! "Good night!" As I got into the back of the car, Diane told me that she was so proud of me. The Wall Street guy asked, "What are you? His mother?" (He doesn't know how right he was!)

Another time at Mar-a-Lago with Diane, enjoying people watching and trying to act the part: I got lucky by being introduced to a couple of beautiful women. Cutting one away, I was left with this tall, blonde beauty by the name of Kay. She came across as a little snobby, but that's not so bad. The best part of the meeting was that she lived just down the street from my apartment. The difference was, she lived in a mansion on the ocean. I asked her if she would like to go out to dinner? Her answer was that she was leaving for Europe for the summer. I took that as a kiss off. About four months later, while I was walking to my apartment, I heard a horn blow from the traffic on A1A. A black Mercedes pulled over to the side, and it was Kay. I guess she just got back from her Europe retreat. I hesitated and thought, I guess she wants to talk to me so I ran over and welcomed her back. She looked great! I blurted out, are we still on for dinner? She picked up her datebook and gave me a tentative date. It wasn't the enthusiastic response I was looking for, but what the hell.

After leaving her I started thinking about what would we do, and where would we go. The bulb finally lit up, I would have a boat taxi pick us up on the Intracoastal side of my apartment and have it take us to a waterfront restaurant. That might impress her. This meeting was something I knew wouldn't last, from my past experiences, because of her class and boring lifestyle. Lets see where it goes, that's the exciting part. She was impressed with the restaurant experience and so was I. After that I was invited to her home to see what she was paying $10,000 per month maintenance for. After looking around the compound I could see why. The stairway was like the one in the picture "Gone With The Wind." She definitely, in my mind, was hinting to me to help her with her maintenance problem, so I used that for a reason for cutting short our relationship.

Chapter 25: Pompano Golf Course

Pompano golf course was the closest course to the Hillsborough Mile apartment. It's where I met lots of girls who I played golf with, most of whom could beat me. I hooked up with this one girl, a Korean. She was a great player. She invited me to dinner at her apartment. I told Diane, and she had a fit saying that they eat dogs. Don't go, but I did, looking for dessert. At dinner she did offer me something in a bottle that was from her hometown in Korea. I tasted it, but my mind said it was dog, no matter what it was. Now it was time for dessert in

bed.

There were other girls who I played golf with. One was a young beauty that was 20 years my younger, and her name was Rose. All the guys flipped over her. She loved to go bar hopping and order a bottle of champagne. She paid for the second one so she certainly wasn't using me. One of these barhopping nights, after the second bottle of champagne, she asked me if I would take care of her and I quickly answered, "I am looking for someone to take care of me." At least I was in the running.

My Next Door Neighbor

Judy was a teacher from Detroit, Michigan. She would come down for the two months of the summer when school was not in session. Judy loved the beach. We got to know each other since she lived next door to me. She invited me into her apartment for a drink. I remember sitting at the table in the living room, talking with her. Thinking why beat around the bush, out of nowhere I blurted out, would you like to go to bed together? She agreed, to my surprise. That took care of the summer. We then made plans to meet in Detroit.

My daughter, Jessica, was living just outside of Chicago at this time. I went to visit her, going on to Detroit to see Judy. Her house, which she obtained during a divorce, was very large. Then we went on a tour of Detroit, then up to the Grand Hotel on Mackinac Island. From there we continued north into the Upper Peninsula which I never heard of before. She had a cabin on a lake. It was beautiful country and another life experience, but Judy was geographically undesirable.

June

When returning from Michigan I received an invitation to play golf with Diane and her friend, June. After we played, Diane said she had to go to a meeting. June asked me if I wanted to go with her to look at some real estate. I agreed to go. June was widowed, with two children, a boy, 16 years old and on drugs, and a daughter who wanted to be an actress at 14 years old. June sold Waterford crystal and very expensive china. It was a business her husband built before he passed away. The orders came to her via fax. The business took her periodically on travels all over the world to make appearances. June also belonged to the Boca Raton Hotel and Club and invited me to the beach to meet some of her girlfriends. She insisted I wear a black sling shot bathing suit, which I didn't like. After putting it on I felt I needed a sock in it, but I did it anyway. When we arrived at the beach, two of them were already lying down on the blankets on their stomachs with their tops off. I thought to myself, this is going to be fun. She introduced me. The girls turned to me holding their arms over there exposed chests and greeted me. It's like being back with Playboy! I laid down on my back, and started to soak up some of the sun. This is living! All of a sudden, the sun went away, like a cloud had covered it. I opened my eyes, and to my amazement, it was too big boobs hiding the sun. It was another of June's girlfriend's. What a day!

It was time for June to make a trip to Puerto Rico to see one of her clients. I decided to go with her. While passing time at the Miami Airport, we were sitting at a counter having coffee when I looked over my shoulder and saw "the walrus," golfer, Craig Stadler. I caught his eye and asked him how he had done? He gave me a thumb down. I turned to June and told her who he was. The next thing I knew, I had a tap on my shoulder. It was Craig. He wanted me to know that he had had a good time, nonetheless. In all the years that I have seen Craig play, I don't think he has ever had a good time, but it was a fun experience!

When we arrived in Puerto Rico, it was rather dull, until we went to the casino. I went to the crap tables. I didn't care for gambling but it killed time. I was up about $85.00; we walked away from the table, and went to dinner, paying with my winnings. June couldn't get over how one could walk away while winning. The next morning we went back to the table. No one was there except two men in tuxes. June expressed that she wanted to play. They said, "fine." She didn't know what she was doing, but it was fun watching. She bet against herself, throwing the dice off the table the first throw. She started to win by losing. She got ahead about $100 and walked away. (Figure that one out?) I guess she learned something?

When we arrived back in Florida, I moved in with June, things were going well until the phone rang at about 1 a.m. It was the police informing me that they were holding June's son on A1A in Boca and before they did anything, they wanted to notify his family since he was underage. We got up and drove to the sight. It seems that someone on the beach went swimming and left their wallet in their shoe. The kids came along and seized the opportunity to take the wallet. There were two boys and one girl. They ran to their car, which was parked on A1A just off the beach. There they found the police ticketing their car. The man who owned the wallet hollered to the police as he came running up from the beach. The girl and one of the boys ran off. June's son had no choice but to stay since it was his car. His mother had given it to him after he totaled the other new car she gave him. That's a spoiled brat!

That's when the police called the house. When we arrived at the scene, June's son was out of control. The police told us that they could take his car and throw him in jail, but since he was a juvenile, they called us. They were nice. Meanwhile, the kid was hollering that he was innocent. I told the police I would take care of him, trying to tell him to keep quiet, they're letting you go. He wouldn't stop yelling. He called me a son-of-a-bitch. I grabbed him by the neck and tried to get him in the car. He started yelling yo! yo! The police saw what was happening and ran to my side. They wanted to throw him in jail. I told them that I'd take care of it and pushed him in the car. The police backed off and we got out of there as quickly as we could. June took his car home. (What am I getting into!) She didn't even discipline him.

Ski Trip

June rented a house in Aspen, Colorado, for the New Years Holiday. I decided to go at the last minute. This meant I had to travel First Class, as Coach wasn't available. It cost me $1,500 round-trip from New York, as that's where I was at the time. First Class was great! Geraldo Rivera was sitting behind me. When we got into Denver, we had to take the American Eagle flight to Aspen. Everything was going fine. We were just about to land. I could see the field under me. The next thing I knew, we pulled up and headed back to Denver. It seems the wind was too dangerous to land. So there I was, back in Denver. One guy was frantic. He had a party to go to that evening, so we rented a car and left with two other girls who needed a ride. Off we went, over the hills and winding roads in the dark, of course it started snowing. The driver told us to sit back and hold on. One of the girls was so frightened she wanted him to stop and let her out, but he wouldn't. He had a party to make. I tried to go to sleep, but a few times I thought we were going off a cliff for sure. We didn't! It was frightening!

When we arrived, I found the house and June. It was a nice two-story house. The next day we met with 3 other girls. They were all good skiers. We only had four ski passes, so I was left behind because I was the weakest skier. They intended going to the top of the black. This was the most difficult course. It was suggested that I go cross-country. (And I'm a macho guy!)

It was December 29th, my birthday, so I went to the bar where all the non-skiers hang out. One of the guys there was also celebrating his birthday. Everybody was buying drinks and singing "Happy Birthday." It was a blast! I loved these skiing trips! The next night we were at a restaurant and guess who came in? Diane and Reva dressed to the hilt with their full Texas outfits, boots and hats. I went over and talked with Diane. I thought that they had just come from a costume party, but no, it's just the way they had dressed, representing Texas. Diane was pissed at June for some reason or another. Diane had a young blonde escort with her who didn't say a thing. Maybe he took my place. The next day I ended up with the flu and was sick in bed. June went merrily on. When she returned, she got in bed and wanted sex. It almost killed me, but I did it. June was in the bathroom when the phone rang. I answered. The caller asked; "Is June there?" I said, "no." June had given her phone number to some guy. (Shit! That did it! I'm gone!) I was always suspicious of June's sexual ways.

One time she told me a story about a girl in Puerto Rico that went like this: she was in a cab, she was definitely horny and threw caution to the wind asking the cabdriver if he knew of any man who had an exceptionally large genitalia. He said he did (how the hell did he know), but the story goes on. With a quick call it was ok'd. She told the cab driver to take her

187

there. When they arrived a black man appeared dressed like a witch doctor and was endowed with a 12-inch genitalia. It was one of the best sexual experiences she ever had. I think this girl was actually June, knowing how oversexed she was. Interesting. We finally broke up - the novelty was over. (It was an ugly situation anyway.)

Chapter 26: Bobby

One of Diane's friends told me she had the perfect girl for me and arranged a blind date. I was to pick her up at her home in Tamarack, Florida. She was a petite little blonde, very shy and quiet; just the way I like them. The meeting went well. She told me the story of how she was looking up the street for the car when a little Toyota with a flower on the antenna was coming along. She thought, "Please no." It went by. She sighed. Then I came down with my Corvette, that's more like it! Her name was Bobby. It wasn't long before I moved into her house. She thought it was great that I could repair most things around the house. It was like a hotel with a tennis court and a pool in the back. There was plenty to do. I liked that. The country club she belonged to was mainly a Jewish golf club. They accepted me fine. Bobby wanted to meet my family, so we drove to New York. We stayed at Lisa's house in Garrison, New York. The guest room that we stayed in had a separate bathroom. Bobby broke down in tears because she didn't have her own private room. I guess that's a Jewish princess for you. I told Lisa we were going to a hotel. Lisa was ok with it. She understood.

Coming back from New York, driving southeast on Route 77, heading for Charlotte, South Carolina with Bobby driving, the roads were crowded on both sides. We were following a van on the right lane. It was a concaved, divided highway, about 50 yards between the north and southbound lanes. I noticed a cloud of dust on the north side lane about 100 yards ahead of us. A car started coming down the concaved divider, not losing any speed. I could see that the car was going to be airborne right at us. I told Bobby to turn left, in a firm voice, onto the left lane and if we had to go down into the valley, we would. This was happening very fast. The on-coming car became airborne and flew in front of us, hitting the van that we were behind. The airborne car started spinning like a top and missed my window by a foot. It spun into the path of a 18 wheeler and was flattened out like a pancake behind us. We pulled over, I ran out of the car to the van that was in the woods, turned over. There was a woman climbing out of the roof with a baby in her arms. She said screaming, "I think my mother is dead." Her father was thrown into the woods against a tree. He said, he couldn't move, I helped the daughter out through the back of the van. After pulling everything out, I told her to take care of her father. The truck that hit the spinning car kept going. I guess he didn't want anything to do with the complicated accident. There was money all over the place, like leaves blowing around. People started coming from other cars to help. The mother was dead. Finally, I could hear the sirens of the emergency vehicles in the distance. That was when I left for my car, Bobby, who was still in the car was badly shaken. We drove off, not talking for quite a while. I felt that this incident brought us closer together. I can still see that car twisting in the air by me today. Just moving into the left lane, saved us. I still think basketball, and judging distances helped. When we returned to Florida, more bad news, Bobby's mother had a heart attack and was in the hospital. We went up to see her. She was a great woman. At her bedside I gave her a kiss, knowing that she loved it and got a little smile from her. Bobby said that always worked. I left the hospital and Bobby stayed with her Mother. It wasn't long after when she passed away. This is the hard part of life. But in death there are sometimes rewards. At the

reading of the will, she didn't forget me and left me her Cadillac. She knew I loved it, bright red with a beige vinyl top. She always bragged that she paid $50,000 for it. Right after that, Bobby decided to sell her house and have a new one built at Marisol Country Club in Palm Beach, Florida. The builders arranged for her to stay in an apartment that was near the sight of the construction. That left me in a predicament. I wanted to be near my work. We decided that I would get my own apartment. It was about 20 miles from where she was living. This made me realize that I wanted us to get married. I asked her and she said, "yes!"

We made plans to be married on the sixth hole at Marisol, next to the new house. Everything was going fine until Bobby told me that she thought it would be better if I stayed in my own place and we would see each other. Like usual I thought to myself, that something was wrong. She didn't give me a reason. I believed it was that she had come into a lot of money. That changed a lot of things. She did tell me that she thought she was going to lose me. All I could say was, "goodbye." I never called her again and she didn't call me. I decided that all the awards and trophies had just become a drag each time I left a girl, so with a little sadness; I packed up three large garbage bags full and dropped them into the garbage. On with life!

Fun House

Not far from the Ritz-Carlton (in Manalapan, FL) I bought a house for an investment. It became a great party house. The decorators who I worked for or did business with donated almost everything in it. I put in a large sit-down bar and satellite TV to see all the fights and shows, but the best thing was the back patio. It was a 20 x 60 foot room with an in-ground Jacuzzi, a rug that made for great putting contests and at some of the parties we even had some professional golfers try their abilities. I hated to leave the beach apartment, but I needed more room. I missed calling a water taxi to take my dates to a restaurant and having them pick us up a couple of hours later to take us back. That was always impressive. When having parties at the new house, I had to separate my golfing friends from the high society ones. They just wouldn't mix together. Live and learn.

I went right back to Diane, like a homing pigeon. She would drink and talk about the things we were going to do together. Things like taking a trip up the Intracoastal on a fancy yacht, stopping and playing golf, tipping heavily so everyone would remember us, picking up different friends at other locations. The next day she would forget what she had said.

One evening we went to a restaurant and on the way home, while I was driving, Diane started rubbing my leg and didn't seem herself. When I was dropping her off, she pleaded with me to come up to her apartment and stay overnight. I didn't know how to handle it because of all the years of being friends with no sex. I chickened out and said that I had to get up early for work and drove off. I think with some satisfaction or, maybe, I felt I couldn't satisfy her.

Downfall in L.A.

Diane asked me if I wanted to go with her and the girls to LA to play golf and party. I agreed to it. The change would be good. Just so you know, I paid for my own plane ticket and golf, but I did stay at their rented apartment on the ocean. On the trip it was Diane, Reva, Nicki and Diane's business advisor. We played all the best golf courses and went sightseeing, at all the LA things. It was a coincidence that my daughter and her husband, Lisa and Charles, were in LA at the same time doing a tape on Yoga.

We got to have dinner with them, a cookout at Diane's apartment. It was great! I cooked and burned the chicken. What's new? The next night the girls were going out to dinner. I decided not to go, because I was going to leave the next day and wanted to get organized, knowing that they were going to get plastered. When they returned, around 2 a.m., Nicki crawled into bed with me. I knew this wasn't good. We started making a lot of noise and Reva stormed into the room, calling Nicki a bitch and me a bastard. She said Diane is in the next room crying. She also told Nicki she was fired. She told her to get out of that bed. Nicki looked at me and I told her to stay right there, Reva waited a minute. She saw that her demand was not met. Reva left the room. We had a hard time going to sleep, but our butts were stuck together like glue, finally falling asleep. The next morning we got up early and walked on the beach, talking about the past night, then stopping at Starbucks for coffee. I noticed one thing about LA. Bums all go to Starbucks. I could never figure that out. Getting back to the story, we went back to the apartment. Everyone was up, we greeted one another and not a word was said about last night. It was a little uncomfortable, so I got my things, hopped in a cab and flew back to Florida. I then found out that Nicki did get fired. Reva called me and told me that Diane misinformed her about our relationship and she was very sorry for the way she acted and still loved me. I said the same. I called Nicki a couple of times, but our fun filled relationship again faded away. I sold the house, made a few bucks and retired from work. I guess, in a way, I was hurt and just wanted to get away from everything.

Chapter 27: Palm City

Dick and Milly invited me up to Palm City, Florida. They had a house with servants' quarters that they let me use. I had access to boats, fishing, with plenty of projects to keep me busy. Dick and Milly had several people working for them on a 17-acre parcel of property with 40+ goats, miniature horses, black swans, ducks, turkeys, chickens and other critters. I then had my father come down from New York to enjoy the warm weather. I also bought him a three-wheel bike that he enjoyed riding for the month he was here. Then he returned to New York. One of the girls, named Rosie, who worked for them, was an ex-truck driver with a big set of jugs that she would throw around in her T-shirt. She always said she would kill me if she ever got me in bed, but she had a boyfriend working there also, thank God. I needed that like a hole in the head, but she did tell me about a bar and restaurant with a dance floor that I should go to where I might meet someone. I hesitated, but considered maybe it was another road in life. It was a first class restaurant and bar with a live band, so I went in. I walked into the bar area. There was a nice crowd. I ordered a drink. Next to me there were two women who were talking about golf, while watching it on a TV set over the bar. I got involved in the conversation and introduced myself as Richard Bennett. Their names were Connie and Loli. Connie replied, spelling out my last name B-e-double-n-e-double-t. She told me; that is my maiden name and we might be related, but no! I told Connie that I had been married three times. She returned that she had been widowed 20 years. I guess that evens things out? I began telling her about my life, which was hard for her to believe. There's more to life than we think or is it fate that brought us together that night? Connie had been a music teacher at Brookside School / Cranbrook, North Bloomfield Hills, MI. This was a very exclusive private school. Connie played piano beautifully. She introduced me to church, where she sang and was an elder. One of the first sermons I listened to was: Quote

> "The Bibles description of a man of ill repute, found in chapter 2 Timothy: 3:6-9 quote: 6) they are the kind who will worm their way into homes and gain control over weak-willed women, who are loaded down with sins and are swayed by all kinds of evil desires. 7) always learning, but never able to acknowledge the truth. 8) just as Jannes and Jambres opposed Moses, so also, these men oppose. The truth-men of depraved

minds, who as far as the faith is concerned, are rejected. 9) but they will not get very far because, as in the case of those men, their folly will be clear to everyone."

(After hearing that I wondered, was that me in the past?) But I did find another reason to go to church. As I entered the chapel, finding my place to sit, I would begin to think of my mother and friends, those who had passed away. In the silence of my thinking I would say" hello," to them, hoping that there was some way that they could hear me. It seemed that I was in the right place to make that contact. And it made me feel good!

Marriage # 4 (2005)

Connie lived in the Martin Downs County Club community in a nice house. After a year of dating, we decided to try living together. She told me she didn't have enough closet space for me, so I added a closet and expanded another, which took care of that. With the closets settled and a year of getting to know one another, I decided to propose to Connie... She thought it over for a day before she gave me her answer "YES". Then we got married in Palm City at the Presbyterian Church by Pastor Dick Anderson.

Connie graduated from Michigan State. She has two sons Eric, a graduate of the University of Michigan, and Rob, a graduate of Purdue University. "Boy they must've had a good rivalry over Big Ten sports." Eric has two girls, Madison, and Riley, plus a beautiful wife, Vickie, who received her degree in teaching. Rob has two daughters, Torie, Erin, and one boy Tyler. We can't leave out his dynamic wife, Kelley. They all accepted me as G-pa, short for grandfather. That's what life is all about and what to look for in a partnership that will last. All the roads that I have taken, led me to finding out what is the most important thing in life, and that's not money or fame, but the love of a family. (Family is everything!)

Back to Diane

Diane and I didn't talk for two years until Reva called and told me that Diane's daughter was getting a divorce and her mother was ill and would I call her. I did, she was happy to hear from me. She invited my new wife, Connie, and me to stay at her house for a couple of days in Boca Raton. It was on the Intracoastal Waterway, and we could catch up on things. I called Diane's house to make sure everything was ready for us, knowing her from the past. She can be unpredictable. I talked with the maid; she didn't know where Diane was. It was just like old times, but she finally called. It seems that she had a surprise birthday party that went like this. Reva called Diane, and informed her that she had to come to the airport to look at a new Learjet to buy. Diane said no way, the one we have is fine, but Reva enticed her with some good prices. It turns out that there were 10 of her girl friends hiding on the plane, surprising her by singing happy birthday. They took the plane to the Bahamas, where she said she lost her shirt gambling and partied heavily. She made it back in time to meet us at her house, which had an elevator and servants; Andy Warhol pictures, Rodin's, 550 Mercedes and a Aston Marten black convertible (not bad). We went out to dinner with her mother and father, whom I loved.

196

(Her mother was in good health…?) Then we had dinner the next night at her home. She did ask me if I was happy. I said, "yes," she wanted us to stay another night, but both of us had enough. It was great, but still not real. We left on a good note, but her world is not for me. I'll never forget all the good times we had, but I realized, that I prefer the simple life. I am glad that Connie could see the life that I had left.

DAD

I knew this day would come. My father, after 101 years, finally passed away. He just fell asleep and didn't wake up. What a way to go! I can't say enough about my two sisters, Barbara and Pat, also Fred, my brother-in-law for making my father's last years so comfortable with love and care. I hope we all have a great ending like that. He was my buddy.

My father also retired from American District Telegraph, collecting a pension from them until he passed away at 101 years of age. Thank you, A.D.T.

A few months later, my sister's husband, Fred, was very ill and was given a few days to live. I immediately made arrangements on a flight from West Palm Beach. The plane was on time, but it seems one of the crew members got ill on the incoming flight. The captain decided that without a full crew he would cancel the flight, and that left me in a no-win situation to make my change in Atlanta. There were no other flights going out, so they finally gave me a free flight, round trip that would leave in two days. Of course, Freddy passed away. That's just about how things go.

I finally made it up for the funeral, with a nice Marine tribute at the funeral. My cousin, Gina, was there. She was the one I met in the city who works for the phone company and gave up her life to take care of her mother and aunt. It was the last time I would ever see her. She was a beautiful and wonderful person. All the good ones are going. I'm starting to see all my friends and relatives dying all around me, I'm beginning to accept that one day I am going to die. You know what I mean, for example, motion pictures. You watch one of your favorite movie stars for years, growing older and finally dying, but you haven't changed.

Chapter 28: Fishing Camp

One day in the mail, Connie received a tax bill for two acres that her father had left her many years ago in his will. I was curious about the location. I looked it up on the map. It was surrounded by some of the best fishing lakes in Florida, which I loved, so we decided to go look for it.

It was near Daytona Beach, but inland. The roads were dirt and washed out, too rough to drive, so we gave up. A couple of months later, we decided to try again. This time we asked real estate people in town about the area. They gave us aerial maps, which showed us that the two acres were across the road from a trailer home. That gave us some bearing on location. They did tell us that we would need a four-wheel drive vehicle to get back there, but we went anyway. We found it, estimating distances from the aerial shots, and the trailer across the road. It was like a jungle with a culvert 10 feet wide. You couldn't get over to the property by car, so we would have to build a bridge. We did try to walk, however, we could only get half way into the property. We returned home and I thought, what a great fishing camp it would make. I started thinking about the trip up there, which was 150 miles. I would have to clear the area, build a bridge plus build something to stay in. I called the town, they led me to the code people. They said that if I built a bridge, I would have to put a 24-inch pipe under it to handle the flow of water during heavy rains. They also told me I couldn't build on it, but I could have a trailer. I started clearing the area. It was like I was back on my Uncle's farm in North Carolina with a chainsaw in my hand, cutting down trees that were mostly pine. I remember an old man walking down the road, stopping

and telling me to be careful or they will find you. He was talking about the code people. It seems no matter where

I go I find some kind of a problem. Meaning the woman in the trailer across the road had two kids, Bobby 12, and Nancy 10. They were two beautiful kids and their mother had a new boyfriend every month. Every time I arrived at the property, the kids would be right over. They were a big help in building the bridge. They would always invite me over for dinner, but I

was very careful to let them know that I was old enough to be their grandfather. I didn't want them to think that I was available for their mother. One weekend I finally cut my way to the back of the property with the help of the kids. I found a beautiful creek visualizing a little dock and a gazebo overlooking it. Now I know how Alec Guinness felt when he finished the Bridge on the River Kwai.

I just love the satisfaction of all these projects. I also had a well put in and I purchased a 24-foot trailer with air conditioning, full

bathroom, and kitchen that slept four. Now I needed a generator, I even put flowerbeds to give the area more color.

It's like being a settler, working his piece of land, exhausted at the end of a hard day of cutting trees and clearing the area for

his home. Connie didn't want anything to do with it. It wasn't her thing, much too rural for her. To me it was the greatest feeling at the end of the day just to put your feet up and look out over your work and appreciate nature. That's a real life. I would occasionally take up a couple of my buddies from the country club. They wanted to see my project and do a little fishing. One night, while we were watching TV, there was a knock on the door. It was the kids from across the road and their mother. They both gave me a big hug, like I was their adopted father. The mother came in and was complaining that she hadn't had sex in two weeks. That's all these guys had to hear, you can imagine what they were thinking. After that, the area started to develop fast. They widened the main road and started to build country clubs along it. We started to get offers on the property. One company from California gave us a high bid, so we figured they must really want it. We came back with a higher price, lo and behold, they said okay. It was a good time anyway. The gas was going up in price plus I was getting tired of the 300 mile round trip. About six months later, there was a recession. So we hit it right. It was another education and experience, Connie was happy for me also.

Chapter 29: Madison Square Garden – 2008, the

coach of the Killeen's basketball team, called me and said that the team was going to be honored by the National Pro Am City League Association Inc. at Madison Square Garden for its contribution to New York City basketball. John Andre's was the Master of Ceremonies. He is the voice of the New York Knicks. CEO and president, Cecil Watkins, hosted the affair. Many pros from the NBA, coaches and referees were there. It would be great just to meet all my old basketball buddies and especially in a place that is the ultimate setting in our dreams. After picture taking and a lot of inflated storytelling, it came time for the awards. I was the last to receive my award. Danny Doyle introduced me, expanding on my marrying a Playboy Centerfold and basketball highlights. I noticed that the guys before me receiving their awards would thank their

wives for their support and kind of struggled up the three steps
to the podium. So I was determined that I was going to run
up, praying that I wouldn't fall (and I didn't!). They asked me
to say something, so I thanked my four wives for their support.

That brought down the house. What a way to end my story,

but one more thing
happened. There were
plenty of young college
basketball stars who were
fathered by the group that
were there. As I was
leaving, they wanted to
shake my hand. That was
more of a highlight to me
than anything; a whole new
generation of ballplayers
acknowledging me. I loved
it.

Now, that my life is

an open book for all to see and to judge me, I must admit that most of the time I didn't know if I was doing right or wrong. I just did what I wanted at the moment. (But that's life.)

True Feelings

I always thought that I was a rather unique individual, someone different than other human beings. My life has been both unusual and special. I have lived The Life Of A Player. Now I look into the mirror and see someone who is growing older, just like everyone else, without the wants and desires of youth. But my life isn't over yet; with all my loves I've finally found the real thing.

Now I'll go on to a different kind of life, one with more knowledge and more understanding about life. When I leave this world, I know that I got the best of it.

6/23

Made in the USA
Charleston, SC
13 November 2015